FAMILY TREES

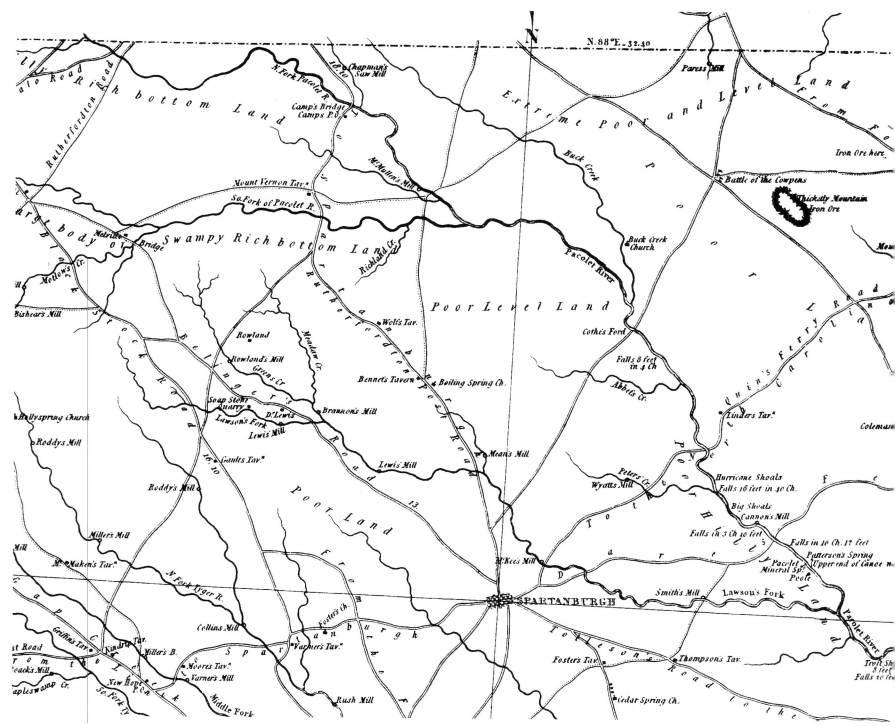

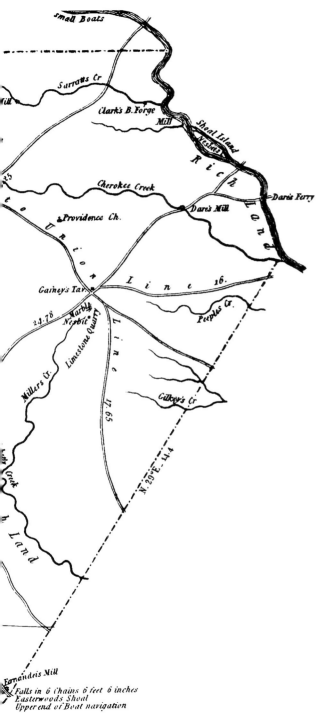

FAMILY TREES

The Peach Culture of the Piedmont

text and photography by
Mike Corbin

New Hanover County Public Library
201 Chestnut Street
Wilmington, NC 28401

19 98

ISBN 1-891885-02-2, softcover
ISBN 1-891885-08-1, casebound
First printing, October 1998

Hub City editors, John Lane and Betsy Wakefield Teter
Cover and book design, Mark Olencki
The reproduction on the title page is a portion of the "Spartanburgh District" map originally produced
    by J. Whitten in 1820 and improved for the Mills' Atlas of South Carolina of 1825. The present-day location
    of Cash Farms is just southwest of "Thicketty Mountain Iron Ore."
Front cover photograph, **Hand of Kline Cash, Red Globe Orchard. July, 1998.**
Back cover photograph, **Early Commercial Orchard, Spartanburg County. 1925.**

Hub City Writers Project
Post Office Box 8421
Spartanburg, South Carolina 29305
(864) 577-9349 • fax (864) 577-0188 • www.hubcity.org

This book is dedicated to
the Cash family and to all
the individuals depicted
on these pages.

in memory of
Donelda Lee

*"Cultivators of the earth are the most valuable citizens.
They are the most vigorous, the most independent,
the most virtuous, and they are tied to their country,
and wedded to its liberty and interests,
by the most lasting bonds."*

—Thomas Jefferson, 1785

THE CASH FAMILY TREE

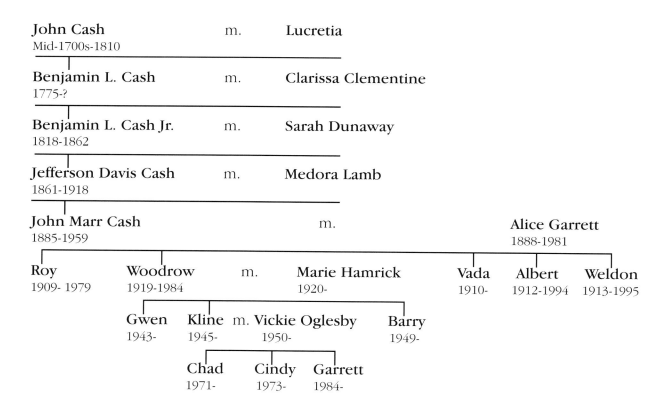

John Cash   m.   Lucretia
Mid-1700s-1810

Benjamin L. Cash   m.   Clarissa Clementine
1775-?

Benjamin L. Cash Jr.   m.   Sarah Dunaway
1818-1862

Jefferson Davis Cash   m.   Medora Lamb
1861-1918

John Marr Cash   m.   Alice Garrett
1885-1959   1888-1981

Roy   Woodrow   m.   Marie Hamrick   Vada   Albert   Weldon
1909- 1979   1919-1984   1920-   1910-   1912-1994   1913-1995

Gwen   Kline   m. Vickie Oglesby   Barry
1943-   1945-   1950-   1949-

Chad   Cindy   Garrett
1971-   1973-   1984-

PREFACE

BY DORI SANDERS

In this fact-filled book, author Mike Corbin not only invites the reader to savor the taste of the glorious peach, but he goes to great lengths to present the relationship of man to the earth. One walks the orchard with Kline Cash, owner of Cash Farms, on the first day of picking after the devastating frosts of the 1996 season and senses the nervousness surrounding the crucial first picking, inspection, and packing. There is trust and experience in Cash's words because the Cash family has lived in South Carolina since the late 1700s and has been farming peaches since "Big John" Marr Cash planted the first peach trees on the family farm in 1925.

To walk with Kline Cash, a lifelong peach farmer, on his family's land is a rare and beautiful experience, as peach farmers are disappearing each year at an alarming rate. Competition from California growers, the rising cost of real estate, perilous weather, and housing and industrial development endanger the livelihood and existence of all peach farmers in the Southeast.

And yet, despite the dangers that come from farming, the farmers and workers hired to pick peaches carry an "unspoken sense of celebration" into the fields. Driven by a love for the land, they work to the rhythm of a music all their own—the "clatter of the aluminum orchard ladder." With threats from nature and man's desire to expand, Cash works his orchards with a fervor that must certainly come from the fear shared by his crew chief Larry Moore who says, "All this, this will be gone someday."

Fortunately for the South Carolina farmers, quality is becoming more important than quantity in the peach business. Although California, due to consistent weather and irrigation, outproduces the Piedmont and all other regions of peach growers, the color, taste, and juiciness of a Southern-grown peach can't be beat. However, gone are the days when the average peach buyer would drive away from a peach shed with two bushels of peaches for canning in the back of the car. Nowadays, most folks want a peach to taste or a small bag. I find this to be true at my own peach stand along Highway 321 in Filbert, South Carolina.

A peach's color, taste, and juiciness are indeed gifts from nature, and they are the children of a farmer's good care. Weather determines all. Cash Farms puts its "heart and soul into it all year long," but, like all farmers, can lose everything to hail, frost, or rain. As Mike Corbin tells us, even back in 1865, Aiken peach farmer Henry William Ravenel had respect for the weather and knew who was boss around the Piedmont when he wrote in his diary, "The peach crop is sometimes lost by early frosts, and having no other means of subsistence, it (peach farming) would be precarious for a dependence."

One can't count on the weather, but there are always one's family and friends and even field workers. Reading this book, one becomes familiar with the trees, the packing house, and the trailers filled with bins. The reader is invited to sit around the peach shed to share the family memories of the first Cashes to grow peaches on this land. And, as the author points out, the reminiscences "are still as fresh as the peaches hanging on the branches of the trees."

The best peach is the result of so many things—the land, the weather, the farmer, the trees. But just as the weather can affect the crop, the marketplace also determines the life of the peach farmer. Even Cash admits, "It is not enough to have grown and gathered the best possible fruit. (You) have to sell the peaches too." Competition forces the peach farmer to try new ways of selling his peaches. Changing with the times, the perishable-fruit mail-order business is something Cash is willing to try.

With so many things that can go wrong on the farm—and so many things that do go wrong —what makes Cash and the others head out into the orchard each morning? Cash's neighbor, 85-year-old Miss Hatchette, a lifelong peach farmer, offers a possible answer when she says, "My heart was in the peaches. It was my life." It is so sad when a changing marketplace makes some peach workers "outlive the peaches on the farm."

However, the reader comes to truly believe that Cash will always be "on the seat of the tractor." His footsteps in the orchard, morning, day, and night, convince the reader of this. And if that isn't enough, his words, "tree-ripened" from a lifetime on the land, are the real thing:

> "The reason I stay here and farm is just to put a seed
> in the ground and see what you can make it produce.
> That's the bottom line, just watching things grow, to
> be close to nature."

In the end, *Family Trees* invites the reader to walk the orchards and take a peach!

Dori Sanders, the author of two novels and a cookbook/storybook, lives and writes on the 200-acre peach farm in York County, South Carolina, where she grew up.

PICKING PEACHES

Thursday, June 19, 1997

Kline Cash is in the middle of his farm's Harvester peach orchard. It is just after 7:30 on a beautiful summer morning, and the sun has begun to warm the air. Kline is walking through the orchard, talking to the men he is paying to pick his fruit and inspecting the peaches on his trees. This is the first day of picking of the 1997 season, a crucial time for Kline and Cash Farms. In 1996 a severe cold spell in March all but wiped out the peach crop, not only for Kline but for the entire industry in Carolina and Georgia. He badly needs a good season this year.

Kline and his crew chief, Larry Moore, remind the men to pick the peaches for background color.

"The background has to be this yellow," Kline points out on a big peach that he has reached up and picked from one of the trees. "It doesn't matter how big it is or how red it is; if that peach hasn't turned yellow, isn't mature, it will never ripen and 'taste' after you pick it. If it's yellow, they'll be ripe in a couple of days."

Larry will periodically call out, "No green stuff!" Nearly all the men in the crew have done this before many times, and few would make so rank a mistake as picking a green peach. Many of them pruned the same trees this winter and thinned them in the spring. Others arrived from Florida just a few days ago.

Cash Farms is at the epicenter of the southeastern peach belt, which stretches from North Carolina to Georgia. The orchards straddle the county line between Spartanburg and Cherokee in South Carolina, not far from a monstrous peach-shaped water tank that towers over busy Interstate 85. The Cash family, whose roots in this area go back to the late 1700s, has been farming peaches on this land since the fruit was introduced as a commercial crop in the 1920s. At one time, Spartanburg was the second-largest peach-producing county in the United States, even out-producing the entire state of Georgia (whose nickname is "the Peach State"). In the 1940s, there were 3 million peach trees in Spartanburg County and more than 200 active peach sheds.

Today, Cash Farms is one of the few remaining peach farms in upstate South Carolina. The ranks of peach farmers here and across the Southeast have been thinned by development, rising land prices, bad weather, and stiff competition.

A lot of rain has fallen over the last couple of weeks, and Kline, worried about brown rot, has been working overtime spraying a chemical on this field to help prevent the fungus. He wants to make sure the pickers throw all the overly soft peaches they find on the ground.

"No soft stuff!" Larry calls out.

The first of the Harvester peaches being picked are big and mostly covered with a deep, rich red color. The "shiners," the peaches grown near the end of the branches that have gotten the most sun and have the highest color, are among those that will be harvested first on this initial picking. The entire block of peaches, about 30 acres, will be picked in a day and a half. The crew will pick more as the remaining fruit matures over the next 10 days or so, making three or four more "go-throughs" before moving on to the next of the farm's orchards to mature—a sizeable block of Red Globes.

The Harvester block of trees is the farm's biggest and one of its oldest. The trees, 14 to 18 years old, are showing their age. Broken scaffold limbs lie on the ground, and spots of dead or nearly dead trees dot the orchard. Despite its age, most of the orchard is healthy, and the trees are filled with dark green leaves, their branches heavy with fruit.

A steady stream of laughter and banter in both English and Spanish rises from the field. Along with that is a constant clatter of aluminum orchard ladders being carried and set up and taken down, from tree to tree. A certain enthusiasm is about in the field on this morning, the first day of the season. Peaches are on the trees, the air is still mild and pleasant, and an unspoken sense of celebration is evident among men who would undoubtedly snort and mock anyone who described it as such. The heat of this day—and of the days to come—lies ahead. For now, the men are fresh, and the wearing, physical repetition of their labor has just begun.

Kline certainly isn't celebrating right now. He's trying to gauge how many peaches he can get off these old trees and what shape they'll be in. Kline is concerned about the cold damage done to the peaches by the late frosts that visited upstate South Carolina in March. Though not as severe as the cold spell that wiped out the Southeast in 1996, the '97 frosts caused serious damage to Upstate orchards. Some local growers were hurt badly. Nearly all of the fruit on the 250 acres of trees that Kline has under lease were killed. The frost also has damaged his 200 acres of trees. The extent of the damage becomes fully evident as the trees' fruit matures. Split pits, soft seams, and other damage is much more extensive in fruit from orchards hurt by the frost. The defects make the fruit unmarketable, except as culls.

"We lost every bit of our peaches early and late—the front end and the back end. I just hope we can get through this with enough to pay all the bills and have a little operating capital for next year," Kline remarks later in the morning.

Kline Cash's farm rests on the gently rolling hills typical of Spartanburg and Cherokee counties in the Piedmont Plateau of upstate South Carolina. In the heart of the heavily developed "I-85 Corridor," the busy interstate linking Charlotte and Atlanta, the area has been growing steadily since the sixties. This stretch is now covered with major manufacturing plants—BMW, Michelin, Stouffer Foods, Hitachi, General Electric, and many others—some of which have been constructed on land once covered with peach trees. Total employment in this area has increased 50 percent since 1986, and the interstate will soon be widened from four lanes to eight. Spartanburg County, once known for its large peach crop, now boasts that it has the highest per capita concentration of foreign industry in the United States. Subdivisions and golf courses now carry the names of the orchards that have been replaced.

Just about everyone admits that there is a limited future for commercial farming in Spartanburg County. With a few exceptions, the farms that seem to be thriving are those that have successfully diversified into real estate and residential development, as the Gramling and Johnson peach-farming families near Inman have done. Steady, continued growth in commercial and residential development is predicted as the land south and north of I-85 continues to be developed. Emory Price, who has been the director of the Spartanburg County Planning Commission for 20 years, foresees "a solid corridor of development reaching five and 10 miles above and below I-85 in place within 20 years."

Increased land valuation will pressure existing farms. Price cites the cost of land near I-85 in the western part of the county as an example. "In the mid-1980s, pre-BMW," he said, "the average cost for acreage in that area was $2,000-$2,500 an acre. Currently, acreage in that area has sold for $68,000 an acre with prime lots going higher."

There were more than 8,000 farms of all kinds in Spartanburg County in 1930. Today, there are less than 1,200. In the past 30 years, more than 50,000 acres in farmland here has been converted to other uses. More telling, the number of full-time farmers has declined to near 300, less than the population of many elementary schools in the area.

Back in November 1996, Garrett Cash, Kline's youngest child, reported that he was the only farmer in his middle school in Cherokee County, the most rural of the counties along I-85 in South Carolina.

"At school today in geography class, I got to stand up and tell everyone about what we do on the farm. We're studying America right now, and we're just at the farmin' stage."

"There's not many farm kids left, are there?" Kline replied.

"The book says only about 3 percent of the population are farmers in the United States."

"It's less than 2 percent, now," Kline said, laughing. "I think the government took the farmers out of the statistics, there's so few of us. I guess we don't count anymore!"

(According to the U.S. Department of Agriculture, the U.S. rural farm population was 4.6 million in 1992, or 1.8 percent of the total population. That was down from 7 million, or 3 percent of the total population, in 1983.)

Back in the orchard, the crew moves steadily through the old trees, each man gathering the "ready" fruit from one tree before moving to the next. Each of the laborers carries an orchard ladder and has a bucket suspended from a strap thrown over the shoulder. The ladders are eight or 10 feet high and light. They've replaced the older, shorter, and heavier wooden orchard stepladders. Instead of the two back legs of a normal stepladder, each of the aluminum orchard ladders has a hollow pole hinged below the center of the ladder's top step. The single back support makes the ladders easier and faster to use on the uneven orchard floor. The pickers set them up quickly, fitting them deeply into the tree. They climb a few steps, picking all they can within arm's reach, then step down and pull out the ladder, the pole banging back against the front of the ladder, and move on.

These old Harvester trees, like all of Kline's trees, are fairly tall, the upper limbs reaching 10 or 12 feet from the ground. Unlike Cherokee County's Sunny Slope Farms, Kline's much bigger neighbor, and some other growers, Kline does not believe in "topping" any of his trees. A nearby block of Sunny Slope trees on Battleground Road is pruned this way. The trees look like they have been given flat-top haircuts; all the branches above eight feet have been trimmed, making it faster and easier to thin and harvest each tree.

"No, sir, we don't top any trees on this place," Kline declares, pointing his finger skyward. "All this up here above the land is free, and I'm going to use all we can."

Ideally, the pickers reach through the branches thick with leaves, selecting, picking, and then inspecting the fruit once more, dropping any that are overly soft to the ground, before placing the good peaches in their buckets. The buckets are more like pouches, with hard-wired, lima bean-shaped mouths, solid bottoms, and collapsible vinyl sides. The pickers are selecting fruit for size and color, leaving small and unripe fruit on the tree.

Peaches are primarily marketed by size. No matter how colorful the peach is or how it tastes, there is little demand for small peaches. The widest circumference along its middle, the "equator" between the stem end and the peach tip, determines the size of the peach. The pickers estimate size by simply eye-balling it. (Pickers who are overly careless or inept in their estimation receive quick correction from crew chief Larry.) Kline has a computerized weigh-sizer on his grading line in the packing house to size the fruit as he packs it.

Most of the peaches being picked today are good-sized, 2-1/2 inches and bigger, but Kline would like to have more 2-3/4 and 3-inch peaches. They bring a higher price, and fewer are required to make up a half-bushel box, the package he uses to sell most of his peaches. The demand for anything less than 2-1/4 inches isn't good.

"They're harder and harder to sell, the 'twos' and 'one-eighths,' and we don't get much for

Larry Moore. July, 1996.

them. Anything less than two inches isn't worth bothering with," Kline reports.

Larry once worked for peach grower Buck Price near Gaffney. After Buck retired a couple of years ago, he and Kline worked out a five-year lease agreement on Buck's orchards, and Larry came to work for Cash Farms.

For years, Cash Farms worked with a crew chief named Florinda, who ran a Mexican migrant crew out of Florida. Short and stout, she always wore a big hat and drove a little all-terrain vehicle out in the fields. There was no need for a crew in '96, and Kline told her this year not to come, that he was going to give Larry a shot at running a field crew for the picking season.

Larry, a tall, muscular man in middle age, has been doing this kind of work since 1981. He lives in a trailer on the south side of Cash Peach Road, and the core of his crew lives in a block house just across the road on the edge of the Harvester field. Up the road, toward the packing house, are four or five more trailers and camp buildings that the migrant workers moved into not long ago. (Kline says, "I didn't call anybody, they just kind of showed up.")

Larry reports that there are 28 men in the field today, many of whom have come from Florida and are Hispanic. "I'm doing good if I can get a man to crew for two or three weeks anymore. They comes and they goes."

Larry is from Lake Charles, Florida. With a small smile, he reflects that he didn't do well in school: "I was in trouble most of the time. Lasted 'til the eleventh grade."

Today, Larry says, "If I had to give one of my children any advice, it would be: Stay in school. You don't want to be doing this. All this, this will be gone someday."

Many of the men picking peaches in the orchard today helped thin the trees in April. In addition to judicial pruning during the trees' dormancy in winter, thinning the trees—the selective removal of most of the young emerging fruit from the trees' branches—has become increasingly important to the peach grower as the demand for bigger and bigger peaches has evolved. By removing most of the budding fruit, the remaining fruit receives more of the tree's limited nutrients and grows larger. One tree with 600 big peaches is worth a lot more than a tree with 2,000 small ones.

Some of the thinning is done by nature. Kline would welcome a "mild" freeze after bloom. A certain percentage of peach buds killed on a tree would save that much time in removing them later. There is also the "June drop" (in South Carolina, it's the "May drop")—the time in late

Danny McCatskill, Pruning. January, 1997.

Thinning. May, 1997.

spring when the tree naturally sheds some of its fruit, usually when the peaches are about the size of golf balls. Natural thinning does some, but not all, of the removal required if the peach grower is to get the optimum size and revenue from his trees, and peach growers have used a variety of thinning techniques over the years.

Kline has tried most of them, including chemical thinners, high-pressure water guns, bats, ropes, and the "tree-shaker." Powered by the tractor's power-takeoff connection, this device has a collar that is clamped around the trunk of the tree and does, indeed, shake the tree. It is quick. The entire operation, including hooking up and disconnecting from the tree, takes maybe a tenth to a fifth of the time that it takes to hand thin, but it is not selective. "Trouble is, you might have all the peaches off some branches and too many on others," says Kline. Consequently, he still prefers to have each tree thinned by hand and figures that it costs between $200 and $250 an acre.

This year, after the 1996 freeze, the trees came back with more blooms and buds than usual, and thinning took longer. One day back in April, while Kline was in this same Harvester orchard with the crew as they thinned, he was asked how long it was taking to thin one of the heavily budding trees. When he replied, "Maybe 40 minutes or so," one of the crew members smiled and said,

" 'So' seems about right. More like an hour."

The time after bloom is a hectic one at Cash Farms. They have about a month to complete the thinning. This year, behind schedule with such a heavy bloom, Kline had a chemical thinner sprayed on some of the trees and hoped for the best. The results he's had from the thinning agent in the past have been inconsistent, but he was running out of time.

The Cashes' "first known ancestor" was John Cash Sr., a Revolutionary War soldier, born sometime around the mid-1700s, six generations back from Kline. As a reward for his 84 months of service as a private in the Continental Line, John Cash received land grants in Tennessee, which he exchanged, plus $10, for 640 acres on Cub Creek in Person County, North Carolina. His son, Benjamin, born in 1775, migrated from North Carolina just before the turn of the eighteenth century and was the first Cash to appear on the census for Spartanburg County, showing up in 1800.

Situated on a wide ridge between the Broad and Pacolet rivers, this land has been farmed by generations of the Cash family. When Kline's great-great-great-grandfather Benjamin arrived, he was entering what was still regarded as the "back country" of South Carolina. Most of the original settlers were Scotch-Irish and were looking for untitled land. Many arrived, as Kline's ancestor did, from North Carolina and Virginia, traveling on "the Virginia Path," an Indian path that roughly paralleled the Blue Ridge Mountains. They found a land that was heavily wooded, hilly, full of streams and hillside springs. Cleared, the topsoil on the rich bottomland along the streams was typically a foot or more deep with red clay underlying everything. The earliest colonial settlers were subsistence farmers, growing corn and wheat and raising pigs and cattle.

Benjamin Cash and his wife, Clarissa Clementine, gave birth to four children, including a son, Benjamin Jr., in 1818. He married a woman whose father owned 140 acres in what was to become Cherokee County. There were five children from that marriage, including Jefferson Davis Cash, Kline's great-grandfather. Jefferson's son, "Big John" Marr Cash, born in 1885, planted the first peach trees on the family place in 1925. His son, Woodrow, born in 1919, built up the orchards before handing the farm over to his children, Gwen, Kline, and Barry.

Kline Cash, 51 years old, now heads the operation, and his wife, Vickie, runs the farm's offices. Chad, their eldest, is 26 and has worked full-time alongside his father on the farm since graduating from Clemson University in 1993.

Their daughter, Cindy, helps run the office and the farm's produce store. The youngest, Garrett, is 13 and helps with whatever he can when he is not attending school.

The farm has undergone many changes over the years.

"I guess the biggest change has been mechanization," Kline says. "When I was 10 we still had mules on the farm, still had a milk cow. I can remember going out helping Grandpa feed the mules and milk the cow. There were still sharecroppers on the farm, black families that lived on the farm and worked the fields and got a percentage of the crop, that sort of thing.

"I had asthma real bad when I was a kid. Couldn't even get under the packin' house. I almost died a couple of times when I was an infant from that asthma. My first job as far as peaches, well, there was an old shade tree back in Grandpa and Grandmother's backyard. They'd unload the peaches back there until they got ready to pack them. Daddy'd give me 50 cents a day, and I'd sit out there under the shade tree and scare off chickens. They were bad about getting into the peaches. That was my job.

"Now Garrett, he's 13 years old, he'll sit in the office and run the computer, run off labels, everything. When Chad was that age, we'd already gone into the bin boxes. The old packing shed was torn down. We were pretty much automated then. I think we got our first computer in 1980, 1981, something like that. It was just a PC that Gwen used to keep the books on. Now we have a computerized electronic weigh-sizer, a computerized label maker, and three other computers in the office. We're looking at another system to add on to do complete inventory and payroll. It's a lot different now."

At one time, Kline, his older sister, Gwen, and their younger brother, Barry, all shared in running the farm after taking over for their father, Woodrow. In 1987, after the farm had suffered through several consecutive difficult years due to bad weather or poor markets, the three of them reluctantly determined that, despite their best efforts, they couldn't get the farm to a point where it could comfortably support all three of their families. Gwen and Barry handed over the operation of the farm to Kline. Gwen is now a successful real estate agent, and Barry has his own trucking business. (When asked what he *didn't* miss about the farm, Barry laughed and said, "Always being broke.")

In 1997, Kline farmed about 1,000 acres, half of it leased, with about 200 acres in Spartanburg County and 800 acres in Cherokee County. Wheat, cotton, and soybeans were cultivated, and a four-acre, "u-pic-em" strawberry operation was double-cropped in cantaloupes. Overwhelmingly, Cash Farms' most important crop remained peaches; the fortunes of the farm rise or fall on how well the peaches do, and just less than half of the land Kline farms this year is in peaches.

Two prime assets of the farm are its packing house and marketing set-up. The existing packing house replaced one that was built on the site in 1955. Kline remembers that they began tearing down the old shed "the day after we finished packing for the season" in 1975. The present building, a large, 2-1/2 story, steel and concrete structure, was completed just in time to begin packing for the 1976 season.

Kline says, "I thought that Daddy was making a mistake when he put this building up, but I am glad he did now, 'cause I couldn't afford to put up a building like this now. There is no way. It would be too expensive. We can run 250 bins a day through here, 5,000 bushels of peaches, 10,000 boxes. That's a lot of peaches. We just need the fruit."

The ground floor of the building contains the farm's offices, a kitchen, and the produce store. Taking up most of the backside of the building are two big coolers— refrigerated storage—one that will hold 10,000 bushels of peaches, the other with twice that capacity. The largest space in the center of the building is filled with the

Kline Cash. February, 1996.

machinery used to pack the fruit. Boxes and equipment are stored in a huge, open loft above the packing line floor. An enclosed apartment is also "upstairs," home to Kline's daughter Cindy, her husband, Jeff, and their daughter, Celeste.

Cash Farms has a hard-earned reputation, in the vernacular of the industry, of "packing a good peach." Like most of the growers in the Southeast, Kline realizes that quality is key not just to flourishing, but to surviving in a changing marketplace. He has worked hard over the years to fill the Cash Farms box with only the most flawless of the fruit that they grow.

The farm's broker, Keystone Fruit Marketing of Greencastle, Pennsylvania, typically pre-sells all of the peaches that Cash Farms can produce. The company's founder and president, Bob Evans, declares that "the key word to remember with fruit is quality. We try to handle a top-quality product and only work with growers, like Kline, who think like we do."

In the face of increased competition from California for a shrinking market, the continuing challenge for Kline and other Southeastern peach growers is to consistently produce fresh peaches that are bigger, redder, and better tasting. As consumer tastes and lifestyles have changed, the per capita consumption of fresh peaches has shrunk nearly 20 percent in 20 years, from 11.76 pounds per person in 1975 to 9.48 pounds in 1995.

Buck Price, who closed his packing house after the 1995 season, observes, "People just don't have the time anymore like they used to. We used to have lots of people come by and buy two bushels at a time to can, but we hadn't seen that for a long while. Most people would want just a little bag or a small handle basket."

The largest peach-producing state and the largest peach-producing region on earth is California. It has a longer and more consistent growing season than South Carolina. Cold is not a problem, and neither is rainfall. The orchards are all irrigated. Each year, California's total peach production easily surpasses that of all the other states combined. For years, California has dominated the production of the clingstone varieties of peaches used in processing, annually producing over a billion pounds. Over 90 percent of the canned peaches in the United States now come from California. The state also is the largest producer of free-stone peaches, the variety grown for the fresh-peach market.

"California is unbelievable," says Kline. "It is just phenomenal what they can do out there."

In the past, growers in the Southeast worried little about fresh peaches from California. The distance from the West Coast to the eastern and mid-western markets gave a prohibitive advantage to the regional grower, both in freight costs and freshness. That has all changed. California has increased its out-of-state shipments of fresh peaches from just under 14 million packages a decade ago to 19.5 million in 1996. Years like 1996, when the Southeast lost its entire crop, were opportunities for further California expansion into markets that Southeastern growers had once regarded as exclusively their own.

Kline and the other growers in the region know they must press their advantage of being able to bring a superior product, a fresher, riper, tastier peach to market than California, 3,000 miles away.

As Benji Richter, the head of a large peach brokering firm in Charlotte, says, "Sure, those California peaches that have come into our markets are big and red, but *they eat like sawdust.* They just don't have the humidity, the juiciness our peaches have."

"Tree-Ripe." It's not just a name, it's a very real priority for Kline and other growers. The riper fruit is softer, more easily bruised, and has a shorter shelf-life, but adjustments have been made in handling, packaging, and shipment so that regional growers can press their single biggest advantage over the California imports: taste.

Bob McCurry, a friend of Kline's and a long-time grower and peach marketing specialist for the South Carolina Department of Agriculture, makes the point in eloquent fashion: "Nobody can beat the juicy, luscious taste of a big, red South Carolina peach grown from our rich, red clay soils!"

Kline realizes the value of the reputation he and his family have developed over the years. He had a new half-bushel box developed for the '97 season. The design, with red and blue ink on white board, proclaims "Cash Farms, Inc. Quality Growers since 1925." His broker, Keystone, wanted to put its "Passport" label on the Cash Farms boxes, but Kline refused.

"I've spent my whole life putting out the best peach we could, building what reputation we have. There's just no way I could let somebody else put their label on our peaches."

Two current and long-range concerns of Cash Farms are its size and the weather. The farm is beginning to be hemmed in by development and prohibitively expensive land. Even on the lesser-developed eastern side of Spartanburg County, where Cash Farms is located, unremarkable farmland, when available, is being sold for $5,000 an acre, often more. Each year, as more land is developed and less is available at higher cost, the chances for Cash Farms to expand and maximize its packing house and marketing assets are diminished.

Statewide, the peach industry is shrinking at a

precipitous rate. Today, there are roughly 16,000 acres in commercial peach production in South Carolina, down from 41,000 acres in 1985. Peach production has declined from 480 million pounds to 215 million pounds during the same period. Spartanburg regularly produced more than half of the state's crop of peaches through much of the 1950s and 1960s but now is producing less than a quarter of the state's total. Its production was 42 million pounds in 1995, down from 120 million in 1984.

"Spartanburg County will never be the production region we once were," Kline says. "It used to be Spartanburg County grew more peaches than the entire state of Georgia. The real estate prices now, nobody is going to go pay five or ten thousand dollars an acre and grow peaches on it.

"There were quite a few people back in the late sixties and the seventies who went into peach production without a background in it. The money was good, there were new packing houses being built, everybody was buying new tractors, new spraying machines, putting in underground irrigation, grading land. Banks were loaning money. It didn't matter. 'Man, yes. You growing peaches? Heck, yes, we'll loan you money if you're growing peaches.' The banks just shoveled it out there. Then those freezes started hitting, we were overproducing, people quit canning as much as they used to. There were people who got into the peach business and didn't know much about it. They didn't last long—three, four, five years. The people left in the peach business in the Southeast now, they and their families have been in it two and three generations."

Of more immediate and dire concern to the farm is the weather. Peach farmers in the Piedmont have always gambled on the weather. Hail will devastate a peach crop, and severe frosts in March or April will kill the peaches, literally nipping them in the bud. Henry William Ravenel of Aiken, located southwest of here, made the first recorded shipment of peaches from South Carolina in 1860. In his diary entry for August 26, 1865, he wrote: "My only objection to remaining here is that the peach crop is sometimes lost by early frosts, and having no other means of subsistence, it would be precarious for a dependence." The commercial peach industry in Spartanburg shipped its first loads of peaches in 1924, and the first frost to wipe out the entire crop in the county was recorded in 1927.

Looking north toward North Carolina from Cash Farms, the horizon is filled with an irregular pale blue line that is the Blue Ridge Mountains, the more southerly and milder cousin of the Appalachians. The southern Appalachians have historically served to help shelter the region from the worst of the arctic cold waves that sweep down from Canada. Winters are moderate. Snow, though not rare, is unusual, and schools in the area close at almost any amount of snowfall sticking to the ground. Historically, there are few days of really low temperatures in winter (most folks in the region consider "really cold" to be a drop below 20 degrees), and hard or prolonged frosts after the first of April are uncommon.

"It seems like they were a lot more uncommon than they've been the last 10, 15 years," says Kline. For some reason, weather patterns have been cruel to the Piedmont peach growers for much of the past two decades.

Cash Farms lost entire crops to the cold in 1982, 1985, and 1996. Cold weather caused crop loss of more than 50 percent in 1986, 1987, 1990, and 1992.

"It was the coldest I can remember in '85. It got down to minus 15 degrees. We were at the Peach Growers' Convention in Savannah, and all the pipes burst. The parking garage was covered with ice. Nobody could get in or out of the place," Kline recalls.

The eighties were Cash Farms' plague years. On top of those major losses, over 30 percent of the crop was lost to hail in 1983. While the farm had a good crop in 1981, the market was terrible. Kline recalls that the 1984 bumper crop was accompanied by "the worst market since the early sixties." The only profitable years in that span were 1980, 1988, and 1989.

"I guess the most frustrating part about farming is not knowing if you're going to have a crop or not. Losing a crop is the most frustrating thing. I mean when you put your heart and soul into it all year long, and you're sittin' out there at two o'clock in the morning, and you know that 25, 26, 27 degrees is the critical point, and it's at 28 or 29, and you know that once the sun comes up it's going to drop a little bit more. Or either, late in the afternoon, you see that thundercloud back there, and you say, 'Well, I better check this orchard,' and you drive a mile up the road and the hail is just beating 'em off onto the ground, and you were going to pick there the next day. I've had that happen, too.

"My daddy always said that you had to be prepared for three bad years in a row in peach farming, but he didn't say anything about a whole *decade* like we had in the eighties. And when he said it, times were a whole lot different than they are now. Costs are way up, and the market is not near the way it used to be. I can remember back when we were going strong, back in the sixties and seventies, we would sometimes

J.D. Young, Champion Rodeo Rider. Battleground Road. June, 1997.

get $20, $25 for a box of peaches. It didn't happen often, but you'd see it sometimes. Not anymore. Nowadays, just about every year needs to be a good one just to stay even."

He recalls that 1993, 1994, and 1995 were pretty good. "After those three years, I started to get back on my feet a little bit, and I was beginning to see a little daylight. Then '96 came along and set me back again."

Highway 110, named Battleground Road, travels north out of the town of Cowpens to Highway 11 and the site of the Revolutionary War's Battle of Cowpens. Four miles from Cowpens and about 2-1/2 miles from where it crosses over I-85, Cash Peach Road turns off of Battleground. The packing house and center of the farm is on this corner. Kline and Vickie and their sons live across the road in a house that they built in 1971, just before Chad was born. All up and down this stretch of road is family. Kline's mother, Marie Hamrick Cash; his sister, Gwen; brother, Barry; their aunt, Vada; and Gwen's daughters and their families have homes here.

One of Gwen's daughters, Dianne, and her ten-year-old son, J.D., live just down from the packing house. Dianne is widowed, her husband killed in a car wreck when their son was five.

J.D. and Garrett, Kline's youngest son, will sometimes play together on a trampoline in the side yard between the house and the old barn. At times, a billy goat is tethered to the trampoline.

J.D. has energy to spare and often comes to the packing house to work or play, teamed up with Chad, Garrett, or his Uncle Kline. Dianne's place has a corral and horses. Both Dianne and J.D. ride, and J.D. is an accomplished rider and roper. He competes in rodeos across the state and has won championships.

Kline himself rodeoed some as a young man.

"My rodeoing didn't last but about two years. I said, 'There must be a better way than this.' I was going to get killed doing this. Never did break a bone. Got pretty banged up but never did break a bone. I never did really follow the rodeo circuit. It was just a hobby there for a couple of years.

"Finally convinced Momma and Daddy one time to come see me. I think it was the first indoor rodeo they had inside at the old Greenville Memorial Auditiorium. It's been a lot of years ago. I almost got hurt. One of the horses came out of the ring, and she came down, and I fell on my face and rolled over. Then she came down on top of me with her front feet on my chest and liked to have busted my head. Didn't break anything, but, boy, I sure was sore the next day. Knocked me out.

"All I ever wanted to do besides rodeo is have a chance to grow peaches. I never could ride rodeo any good, but I know I can grow good peaches."

Aunt Vada knows everything about the farm and family. Or at least that's what Kline says.

"Well, I don't know everything, but people around here do call me the 'Bureau of Public Information,'" Vada says and laughs. "When someone gets together a family reunion around here, it seems like they always call me about something. 'Call Aunt Vada. She'll know,' they say."

Vada Cash Sellars is 86 years old. She is the sister of Kline's father, Woodrow, who along with her late husband, Paul, was the first to plant peaches in this region back in the mid-1920s. Her father, "Big John" Marr Cash, inherited most of this property along Battleground Road from his father, Jefferson Davis Cash. She has beautiful white hair, a ready smile, and a delightful laugh. Her eyesight is failing, and arthritis has taken a toll on her slight body. She uses a walker or cane to help her get around. Her small hands are slightly twisted from her affliction, "but don't pain me much right now, not like they used to."

Vada's home is right across from the Cash Farms strawberry patch. On this day, she is sitting at the old, Formica-topped table in her kitchen, looking out across Battleground Road at the berries and the peach orchards beyond.

"When I was growing up, my Daddy had to farm, but we always had a lot of help. We farmed cotton and corn, hay and beans, everything like that. Everything that come along that we thought we could do good in, we did. I was the only girl, and I had to do hard farm work, and housework too.

"The first year Paul and I were married, we lived in a house back over where that pretty cotton is—the house is gone now—but that's where we lived the first year."

Paul is gone now too. After 70 years of marriage, he died in 1992. But Vada's memories of those early years on the farm are still as fresh as the peaches hanging on the branches of the trees.

"I remember one Fourth of July when we had our peach field those few years after we were first married, and I got on my long-sleeved shirt and went out and picked peaches all day. I'll never forget our minister—he lived in the parsonage nearby—came out in his straw hat and picked along with us. Oh, it was hot. I remember being so glad when we finished. I've never picked peaches again.

"From 1927 to 1942 we lived in that house up

Vada Cash Sellars.
Battleground Road. May, 1997.

the road that Chad has bought and will move into. Lord, I hated to leave that house. When we moved up here, I cried and cried and cried. Let me tell you about that house. We farmed, raised cattle and had a good crop one year and made $700. My Daddy told Paul, 'Paul, if you lend me half of your part of that, I'll pitch in the other half and build you a house.' And that's what we did. He built that house up there for $700. We lived in it until we built this one. Then Woodrow moved into that house. Kline was born in it. And now Chad, Woodrow's grandson, my Daddy's great-grandson, will live in it."

Vada and her husband didn't farm long. They chose to make a living selling something other than peaches.

"When we first stopped farming, the first thing we did was go to Gaffney and started making mattresses. We didn't stay there long. We moved back and built us a place where the farm's peach shed is now. Our mattresses were 'Super Sellar Sleepers' and we stayed on until the war, around 1942, when we had to quit. With the war on, we just couldn't get the materials and shut down the factory.

"Then we started up on selling cars. Paul would go up North and bring them down and sell them. He'd bring them back here and clean them up and take them to sales. And he would trade a lot. He was a good trader.

"And then, along then, we lost our children."

Jack Everett was the first to die in 1958. He was 23 and teaching agriculture at nearby Chesnee High School. One day, he was soldering drums together at school, and there was an explosion. There had been a flammable chemical inside. Four years later, Geraldine, a 33-year-old daughter, was killed in a car accident on I-85.

"After that, we just drifted. We just existed, that is all I can say. We went up to Chesnee and had a self-service laundry and ran that till we retired in 1975."

She remembers her son, Jack, planting the fields in peaches just before he died. "Paul looked after it a couple of years, but his heart just wasn't in it, and he wound up leasing it to Woodrow. Woodrow kept the peaches until they got old, and he plowed up the trees. After we retired, Paul would sometimes go up and help run the peach stand."

Today, Vada has seven grandchildren and eight great-grandchildren. Geraldine's daughter, Teresa, lives next door, and Teresa's brother, Mike, lives in the Macedonia community nearby.

"I am getting old," Vada says. "I hope I don't ever have to go to a nursing home. I am lucky to have people help me and get me things. I have had a long life, but I am still not ready to go. I hope to be able to stay here in my home. It's not much, but I am proud of it and love being here."

Out in the orchard, the pickers who are gathering peaches will periodically empty their filled buckets into one of the four wooden field bins that rest on a single-axle trailer behind a tractor in the field. Larry will move the tractor and bins down the grassy lane between the rows 20 or 30 feet, stop, jump off the tractor seat, and inspect the fruit being dumped into the bins, reaching into the big, deep boxes and spreading out the piled peaches with his hands, looking for defects. He throws out any that he finds, calling out when he finds them, "No, we don't want *none* of this soft stuff!"

Another tractor with a load of empty bins arrives in the field as the bins on this first trailer-load fill. The filled bins are tractored over the hill and out of the orchard onto Cash's Peach Road. From there, it is a short trip, just a quarter mile or so, to the farm's packing house where the bins will be off-loaded onto the concrete apron on the north side of the packing house.

Each bin is then picked up with a forklift and "run through" the hydro-cooler, a 60-foot-long, squared-off tunnel attached to the north side of the shed. As each bin of peaches slowly travels through the hydro-cooler over a series of cylin-

drical bars, chilled water continuously drenches the fruit, removing the "field heat" and gradually lowering the temperature of the peaches. When a bin emerges from the hydro-cooler, a forklift takes it into the shed and off-loads it in one of the packing house's two coolers.

Kline plans the season's first run of the packing house Monday and hopes to have a goodly number of filled field bins stored in the cooler by that time. It will be the first time since 1995 that any peaches will have been run through the packing house.

Spraying the Encores. March, 1997.

J.D. and Garrett, Trampoline and Goat. Battleground Road. February, 1997.

Gene McClendon. July, 1996.

High Picking. Red Globe Orchard. July, 1998.

Mike Mastropietro and Robert Williams. June, 1997.

Kline Cash. June, 1997.

Joe Paul and Gene McClendon. July, 1997.

Joe Paul. July, 1996.

Jesse. July, 1997.

ORD Tractor. July, 1997.

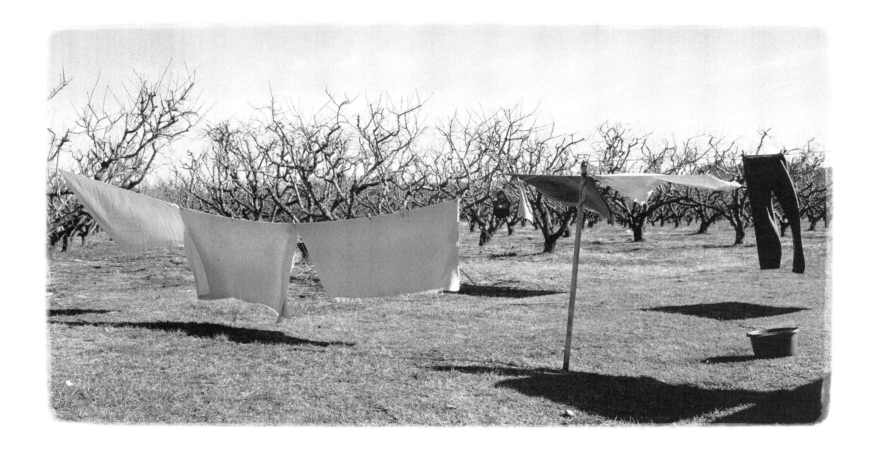

Camp Wash. February, 1997.

Day Done. July, 1996.

PEACH HISTORY

Legend has it that the first peach trees in this section of the Piedmont sprouted from pits spilled from the pocket of a slain British soldier in 1781 in a post-revolutionary skirmish known as the Second Battle of Cedar Spring. Through the years, that battle has taken on a second name and is known in some parts as the Peach Orchard Fight, named for the trees that eventually covered the ground where the soldier died. That legend, of course, is pure fancy, disputed by any number of historical documents that detail the landscape of the southern colonies. Peach trees were well established throughout the South long before the Revolutionary War.

The peach (Prunus Persica) has its origin in ancient China where it was cultivated more than 4,000 years ago. The peach was cultivated in Persia, then southern Europe, and eventually brought to the Americas, first by the Spanish. The fruit spread rapidly throughout eastern North America. By the time of the first English settlement on the South Carolina coast, at Charles Towne in 1670, peaches had reproduced and spread so widely that many thought them to be indigenous to America.

John and Alice Cash surrounded by their children: Weldon, Albert, Vada, Woodrow and Roy. (undated).

Kline Cash on Mule. Late 1940s.

Alice and Chad Cash. 1973.

Mark Catesby's *The Natural History of Carolina, Florida and the Bahama Islands*, published in London in 1712, included these observations of the peach in America:

> Of Peaches there are such abundance in Carolina and Virginia, and in all the British Continent of America, that, were it not certain that they were at first introduced from Europe, one would be inclined to think them spontaneous, the fields being every where scattered with them, and large orchards are planted of them to feed hogs with, which when they are fattened of the fleshy part, crack the shells, and eat the kernels only. There are a variety of kinds, some of the fruit are exceeding good, but the little care that is taken in their culture causes a degeneracy in most. They bear from the stone in three years: and I have known them to do it in two. Were they managed with the like art that they are in England, it would much improve them; but they only bury the stone in earth, and leave the rest to Nature.

John Lawson's account, *History of Carolina, 1714*, included this description of peaches:

> We have a great many sorts of this fruit, which all thrive to admiration, peach trees coming to perfection, with us, as easily as the weeds. A peach falling to the ground brings a peach tree that shall bear in three years, or sometimes sooner. Eating peaches in our orchards makes them come up so thick from the kernel, that we are forced to take a great deal of care to weed them out, otherwise they make our land a wilderness of peach trees. They generally bear so full that they break great parts of their limbs down.

Despite the abundance of peach trees, the fruit was not farmed on a commercial basis during the colonial period because the only urban center was Charles Towne, and peaches were too perishable for exportation.

Peach trees were common in the backcountry, and there were numerous accounts of tribes of Native Americans cultivating the fruit. In the lower Mississippi Valley, a historian recorded that "apple trees, pear trees, and peach trees were reported by some of the French explorers before the establishment of the first Biloxi settlement. As on the Carolina coast, peaches were grown by the Indians in large quantities and were regularly preserved by drying and pressing into cakes . . . the Congarees in Carolina, about 1708, had the art of drying peaches. One large and hardy peach tree was so early and so widely distributed, even among tribes remote from European settlers, that it was called the Indian peach,

Woodrow Cash (right). 1971.

Woodrow, Barry, Gwen and Kline. (undated).

and was thought to be indigenous even by John Bartram, the botanist."

During the second Cherokee War in colonial South Carolina, a militia from the district of Ninety-Six reported setting fire to peach orchards in their destruction of the Cherokee towns of Seneca and Keowee.

By the mid-nineteenth century, individuals in the Lowcountry began experimenting with the first commercial production of peaches in South Carolina. William Gregg, who founded the Graniteville Manufacturing Company to produce textiles in Aiken County in 1847, is credited with having the first large commercial peach orchard in the state, having planted some 8,000 peach trees at his farm, Kalmia. In an 1858 report of the State Agricultural Society, an article by William Summers of Pomaria states that Gregg was "successfully growing peaches for northern markets."

Henry William Ravenel, also of Aiken, shipped peaches in the 1850s too, recording sales to the "Washington market" in New York City. During the Civil War, Ravenel recorded the sale of peaches to a distiller for the making of peach brandy "for the use of the hospitals, State and Confederate." Meanwhile, peach production was beginning in earnest in Georgia, and its crop dwarfed those in North and South Carolina for more than two generations.

J. Verne Smith is generally considered the pioneer peach grower of the Piedmont. A 1951 Clemson University publication declared that he planted "the first commercial peach orchard of any importance to the Piedmont section of South Carolina" in 1901. "As evidence of the fact that Mr. Smith practiced the best horticultural methods, the first trees planted were still producing large crops 38 years later," the report said.

The original Smith orchards on Mt. Vernon Farm were located on high land east of downtown Greer, about 30 miles west of Cash Farms. Smith planted the trees on a hill to keep the frost damage down. Present-day Mount Vernon Road winds and climbs through a neighborhood of spacious, wooded lots and attractive homes. At the very top of the highest hill, in the last house on Peachtree Drive, lives State Senator J. Verne Smith Jr. The stately brick home that he and his wife, Jean, built in 1971 sits at the crest of the land where his father first planted peach trees nearly a century ago.

Verne Smith, aged 73, is a successful businessman and politician. He was first elected to a seat in the South Carolina Senate in 1972 and has been re-elected each term since.

Among the family photographs framed and hung along the staircase in his home is a photograph of the original Mt. Vernon packing house,

Mt. Vernon Farm Packing House. Greer, S.C. 1914.

taken in 1914. A team of mules and two dozen men and boys are posed facing the camera. Baskets of peaches are in the foreground and a few limbs of peach trees come into view on the right side of the photograph.

Seated in the den, Senator Smith has a thick family photo album and a stack of newspaper clippings to go through. As he shares stories about his father and family, he laughs often and obviously has a great appreciation for his family.

"My Daddy grew up on a farm," he says. "His family land was out there at Pleasant Grove—it's about a mile and a half from here towards I-85. He bought this land in four or five different tracts when he was a young man. He set out the first orchard here when he was 25 or 26 years old. He was assistant cashier, working in the Bank of Greer."

The original 100-acre farm had about 70 acres planted in peaches. By 1920, the ex-bank cashier had saved enough money to buy another 100-acre farm in Alto, Georgia.

"This hill here was filled with trees," Smith says, remembering his childhood years. "The trees were contour-planted. The Elberta was our main shipping peach. The first one to come in was the Mayflower, the next one was the Red Bird, then the Carmen, the Elberta, and then the Georgia Belle and just a few Indian peaches for pickling.

"The train depot for shipping the peaches was right here in downtown Greer. Daddy had two big old Percheon horses that he used to haul the peaches to the depot when I was just a little boy. Later, of course, he had trucks.

"Everything we sold was subject to inspection delivery. I heard him tell of times when the market was so bad, he would get a call from New York or Washington, D.C., and they'd say, 'The market is so bad, nobody wants them. We can't sell them for the freight. What do you want us to do with them?' And he said, 'Give them to the Salvation Army.'"

Smith Sr. suffered a heart attack in 1933 while fishing at Lake Murray and died the next day on his farm. He left his wife, Lillian, with five children to raise during the Great Depression.

"When I was 14 or 15, my sister and I had to go down to the Alto farm and harvest and pack the crop," the senator recalls. "We put up the peaches, made the payroll, and hired and fired. I had to go by myself when I was 16. Worked over a hundred people. My goodness, you just do what you got to do.

"What did I like best about growing peaches as a young man? Finishing up and having enough money to pay your debts and make next year's crop. Everything anyone in our family wanted to do that required money, we were told, 'Well, we'll have to wait until after peach season.'"

Verne Smith eventually joined the U.S. Army. After returning from service in World War II, he continued to help his family run the farm and founded a retail tire sales business. Working long hours in the tire store and with the birth of his first child nearing, he got out of farming in 1948.

The Taylor Brothers in Mt. Vernon Orchard. Greer, S.C. 1930s.

"My daddy always talked about building a house here and never got to do it. In my high school annual, they asked me what my ambition in life was, and I said, 'To own a colonial home in the country,' and I got to do it. It was country when we built here, but it's not anymore."

Flipping through his albums, Smith comes across a couple of photos of an old, one-armed man. In one of the photos the man is in a peach orchard.

"That's Mr. Will Holtzclaw. He was born in 1866. He had one arm cut off in a cotton gin. He was our foreman and a grand farmer. We all called him Mr. Bill. When I came home from the war, one year we had a big freeze. Mr. Bill called me and said, 'Let's go look at the peaches and see what got killed.' We came up here and looked at some peaches. Every one we looked at had been killed.

"He said, 'Take me over to Guy Ballenger's.' (Ballenger was another early peach grower with orchards nearby.) I took him over in the A-Model Ford to look at Guy Ballenger's trees, which had all been hit by the freeze too. Mr. Bill said, 'Hell, it ain't as bad as I thought it was. His is killed too!'

"I'll never forget that," the senator says, laughing. "Ain't that a classic! Oh my, when Mr. Bill said that, I laughed. I'll never forget it."

By the early 1920s, farmers in neighboring Spartanburg County began taking a cue from the success of the Smith farm and many others in the state of Georgia. Initially, the commercial production of fresh peaches was an experiment by a few farmers in the northern part of the county who hoped to diversify their holdings. The boll weevil reached South Carolina in 1917 and had migrated to every cotton-producing county in the state by 1920. Volatile markets and bad growing seasons plagued cotton farmers.

In one two-year period, from 1920 to 1922, state cotton production dropped from 1.6 million bales to 493,000 bales, and acreage in cotton cultivation went from nearly 3 million acres to less than 2 million. As Ben Gramling would later say in a 1951 interview, "Our people embarked in the peach game because it was impossible for us farmers to make much money growing cotton exclusively as our money crop, and we had become tired of wearing patched britches."

After preliminary consultations and visits with successful growers in Georgia and agents from the Clemson Agricultural College in December 1920, interested farmers held a meeting at the tiny crossroads town of Gramling on January 11, 1921. A small group of farmers decided to plant what would be the first commercial peach orchards in Spartanburg County. Trees were ordered, and each of the new growers decided to plant five or 10 acres of trees that year.

Many of the men involved in the new enterprise are pictured in an old photograph that hangs on the wall at the Gramling Brothers farm and real estate development office in Gramling, 20 miles west of Cash Farms. The Gramlings have one of the few peach packing houses still operating in these parts. Taken during a pruning demonstration during one winter in the 1920s, the photograph depicts a group of 13 men posed around a leafless peach tree on the edge of an orchard. Not a notably artful or interestingly made image, its significance lies in that it commemorates an event that marks the beginning of an era that would dominate the lives of thousands of people in the area over the next several decades: the beginning of the peach industry in Spartanburg County.

One of the men in that photo is Ben Gramling, whose grandson Henry II now helps run the Gramling Brothers peach farm. The Gramlings' peach orchard is now one-third of its peak size—down to 350 acres—but it is still large enough to support a packing house. Henry Gramling II, 43 years old, is one of several members of the family involved in the diversified Gramling Brothers business. Running the farming side of the business is a job Henry obviously enjoys doing

Early Commercial Orchard, Spartanburg County. 1925.

Toy Hyder. Campobello, South Carolina. January, 1997.

Hyder Packing House. Campobello, South Carolina. April, 1997.

Brannon and Brannon Packing House. Highway 9. March, 1997.

and appreciates, even as he has watched the relative importance of the agricultural part of the family business diminish in relation to other ventures, such as golf course development, subdivision construction, heavy grading, and land surveying.

Henry is happy that the family has done well with its development business but doesn't foresee the family getting out of farming. "It's what got us to where we are. Sure it's a lot tougher than it was 20 years ago to make a profit on our peaches. The costs of labor and of chemicals have skyrocketed compared to what it was. But still, it's a way of life that you just can't replace. It's just part of what we are."

In 1924, the Spartanburg growers helped found the South Carolina Peach Growers Association to help market their first crop. A total of four boxcars of peaches were shipped that summer. It was a modest beginning to an industry that eventually would ship thousands of carloads of peaches annually.

A monument still stands in Spartanburg commemorating the event. Located on the edge of downtown, the monument is modest in size, about 12 feet high, including the pedestal and the stone peach that tops a slab of granite. Erected in 1947 by the Spartanburg Junior Chamber of Commerce, the stone is inscribed on two sides and reads:

An appreciative community
pays tribute to those pioneer orchardists
who through foresight and diligence
established an industry
that means much to our welfare.

They set a worthy example in cultivating
a choice fruit
and their culture of the land
contributed to the culture of mankind.

The first carload of Spartanburg County
Peaches
Shipped July 31st, 1924.

This monument is erected
out of respect for the peach,
delectable fruit of the friendly soil
and a beneficent sun.

Upon a pedestal we place it
as a symbol of God's bounty
and man's enterprise.

Spartanburg County has the honor
of the richest peach harvest in the nation
and we are grateful for this favor.

The peach industry in South Carolina was still in its infancy in the 1930s. Led by the emerging new growers in the Piedmont and in an area of the Midlands known as "the Ridge," production increased slowly at first. Early agricultural census figures included production for both "home" and commercial use, but documents detailing out-of-state peach shipments by railroad car give an indication of the early growth of the industry.

In 1924, South Carolina shipped 91 railroad cars of peaches out of state; North Carolina shipped 1,652 and Georgia shipped 13,513 cars. By 1936, when South Carolina first shipped more peaches (1,285 cars) than North Carolina (934), Georgia was still dominating the eastern market with more than 8,000 cars.

Three million new peach trees were planted in South Carolina commercial orchards in the late thirties, and South Carolina's production increased more than fivefold between 1924 and 1941. In 1946, the state out-produced Georgia for the first time and became the second leading producer of peaches in the United States, behind California. Production in Spartanburg County led the way.

In 1950, there were more than 800 commercial peach orchards in Spartanburg County, each averaging more than 3,000 trees. Nearly 60 percent of the peach trees in the state's commer-

Spartanburg Peach Monument. Erected 1947.

cial orchards were in Spartanburg.

"Spartanburg County produces more peaches than the entire state of Georgia!" was a boast made frequently, if not quite correctly, by area boosters in the fifties and sixties. Peach growers and community leaders joined together to promote the crop and make Spartanburg synonymous with fresh peaches.

One area grower, Paul Black, became president of the National Peach Council, and the city hosted the council's national convention in 1953. (A photograph on the cover of the council's 1953 yearbook shows a giant tissue-paper peach sculpture seated on a raised throne behind the head banquet table in Spartanburg's Memorial Auditorium. The cover also features the Peach Council's credo, "Serving Her Majesty, The Queen of Fruits," a modification from the council's earlier version: "Serving Her Deliciousness, The Queen of Fruits.")

The Chamber of Commerce invited and hosted food editors from cities all over the East Coast and Midwest. The city's newspaper sponsored season-long peach recipe contests and annually published special "peach editions" of the paper. The local minor league baseball team was named the Spartanburg Peaches. During peach season, the posh downtown Cleveland Hotel (now demolished) kept a silver bowl in the lobby filled with complementary Elberta peaches for its

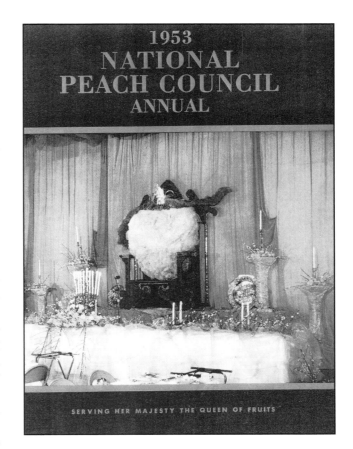

1953 National Peach Council Annual.

guests. The city of Spartanburg began featuring a peach on each of its street signs, a practice continued today.

In its heyday, the peach industry provided seasonal work for tens of thousands of people throughout the Southeast. A farm with 100 acres of trees would employ as many as 300 people picking and packing. For many teenagers, working in the peach shed was their first job.

Spartanburg County's labor pool, even with school out, couldn't provide enough workers, and peach growers imported help from neighboring counties. Polk and Rutherford counties, just above the state line in North Carolina, were a primary source for pickers during the thirties and forties. Many of these pickers were small farm owners looking for work in their slow seasons. Field and shed workers were typically paid 10 to 15 cents an hour.

Howard Painter, a farmer who once packed peaches under the label "Painter's Pride," recalls a short-lived strike in the peach field in 1939. He was a teenager living just outside Spartanburg, working summers picking peaches.

"We didn't have peaches in this area then, so we drove to Inman to pick peaches," says Painter, who eventually became a high school principal. "We picked peaches for 10 cents an hour. In fact, we had a strike to try to get 11 cents. One of the

Field Crews. Spartanburg County. 1930s.

pickers came through before lunch one day and said, 'Look, some of these people are paying 11 cents an hour. What do you think about striking after lunch and see if we can get 11 cents?'

"Cecil Wall and I were picking together, and he said that sounded like a good idea. So, after lunch the crew chief said, 'Let's go. Let's go.' Nobody moved. He kept asking, 'What do you want?'

"The person who instigated the strike wouldn't say anything and just sat there. Finally, somebody said, 'We want 11 cents.'

"Rob McGill, who was the foreman for Dr. Thompson's shed in Inman, said, 'I tell you what. A couple of you come with me. If we can find anybody paying 11 cents, we'll pay you 11 cents.'

"So a couple of us went with him and came back. The long and the short of it was, we didn't find anybody paying 11 cents so we went back to work at 10."

Scene from outside Woodfin Shed. Spartanburg County. 1930s.

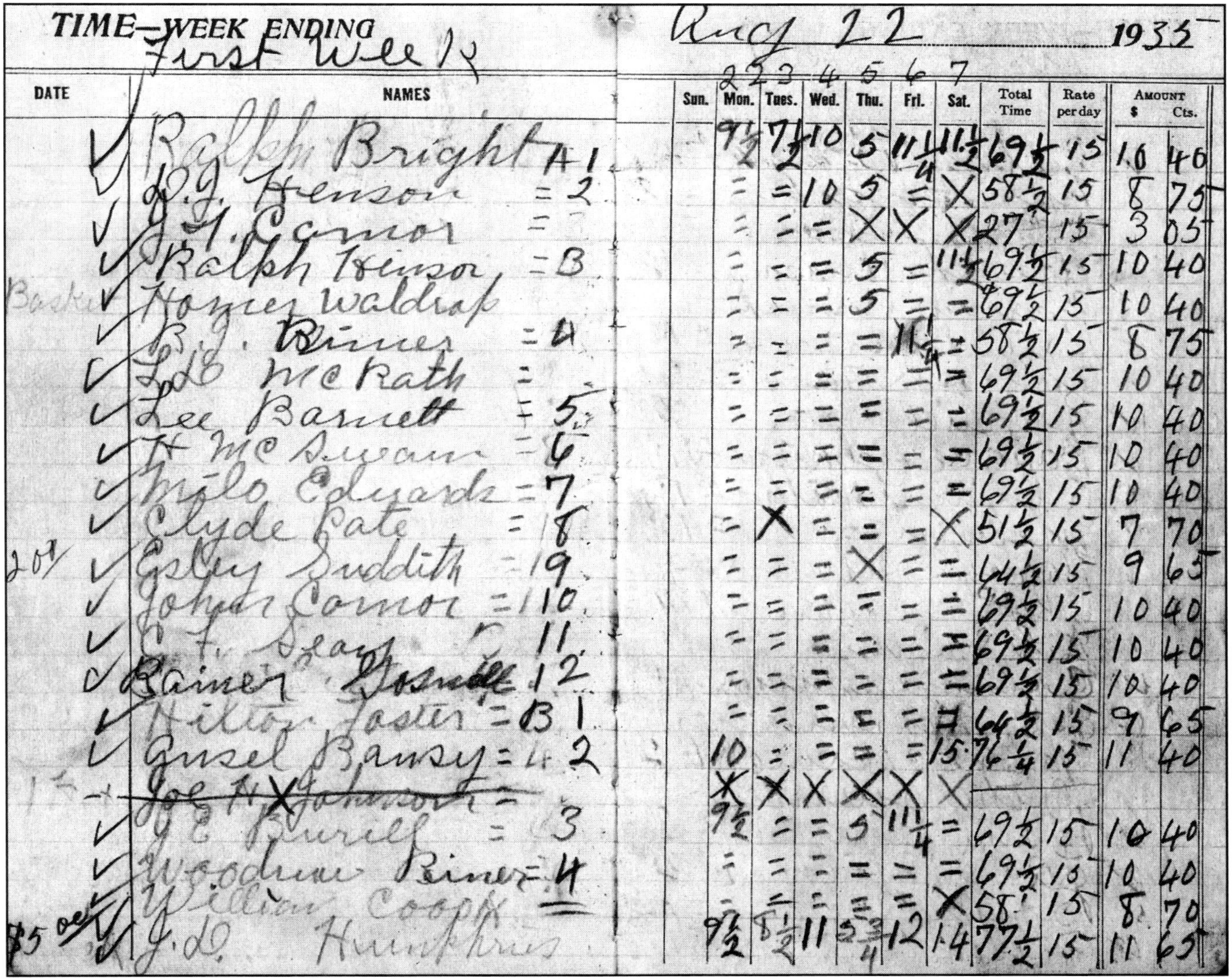

TIME—WEEK ENDING *First Week* Aug 22 **1935**

DATE	NAMES	Sun.	Mon.	Tues.	Wed.	Thu.	Fri.	Sat.	Total Time	Rate per day	Amount $	Cts.
	Ralph Bright A 1	9½	7½	10	5	11	11½		69½	15	10	40
	D.J. Henson = 2		=	10	5	=	4	X	58½	15	8	75
	J.A. Connor =		=	=	X	X	X		27	15	3	05
	Ralph Winson = 3		=	=	5	=	11½		69½	15	10	40
Basket	Homer Waldrop		=	=	5	=	=		69½	15	10	40
	B.J. Rainer = 4		=	=	=	11½	=		58½	15	8	75
	J.B. McRath =		=	=	=	=	=		69½	15	10	40
	Lee Barnett = 5		=	=	=	=	=		69½	15	10	40
	H. McSwann = 6		=	=	=	=	=		69½	15	10	40
	Milo Edwards = 7		=	=	=	=	=		69½	15	10	40
	Clyde Pate = 8		X	=	=	=	X		51½	15	7	70
20¢	Esley Suddith = 9		=	=	=	X	=		64½	15	9	65
	John Connor = 10		=	=	=	=	=		69½	15	10	40
	E.T. Seay = 11		=	=	=	=	=		69½	15	10	40
	Rainer, Boswell 12		=	=	=	=	=		69½	15	10	40
	Hilton Foster = 13 1		=	=	=	=	7		64½	15	9	65
	Ansel Bawsy = 4 2	10	=	=	=	=	15		76¼	15	11	40
15¢	Joe N Johnson =	X 9½	X	X	X	X	X					
	J.C. Burill = 3		=	=	5	11¼	=		69½	15	10	40
	Woodrow Rimer = 4		=	=	=	=	=		69½	15	10	40
35¢	William Coopk =	9½	=	=	=	=	X		58½	15	8	70
5 oct	J.D. Humphries	9½	8½	11	5¾	12	14		77½	15	11	65

Time Sheet. 1935.

For decades, the Upstate region out-produced other regions of South Carolina. But as farming in the Piedmont declined in the 1980s, the middle part of the state became the predominant peach-growing area. Finally, in 1986, Edgefield County surpassed Spartanburg in the number of trees under cultivation and the amount of peaches produced. A brick arch proclaiming Johnston, South Carolina, to be "The Peach Capital of the World" now greets visitors entering town on Highway 23.

Edgefield is part of an area of the state known as "the Ridge." Made up of parts of Lexington, Aiken, Saluda, and Edgefield counties, the Ridge section is slightly higher than the surrounding land. The difference in elevation is critical: the colder, heavier air flows down off the ridge into the surrounding lower lands, allowing the peach buds in the Ridge orchards to survive early spring frosts. Farms on the Ridge are typically much larger than the remaining Piedmont orchards: Clark DuBose of Ridge Spring has 2,600 acres under cultivation, and the Younce Farm outside Johnston has roughly 2,000.

The Sandhills area of South Carolina, northeast of Columbia, has traditionally produced large numbers of peaches, but the number of orchards is declining rapidly there too. The Sandhills, though, is the home of McLeod Farm, recognized by many growers as the best-run and

"I am a tree!" Kline Cash at Watsonia Farms. Moneta, South Carolina. January, 1997.

most modern in the state. The McLeods first planted trees in 1916, and now some of the newest technology in the industry is tested on their farm. There are some bigger peach farms in South Carolina, but few approach the McLeods' reputation for quality. If peach farming is to survive in South Carolina, some say it will be determined by the success of the methods being used by Kemp McLeod and his sister, Beth.

The farm is headquartered near McBee, in a sparsely populated area of Chesterfield County where farmland sells for as little as $500 to $1,000 an acre. The McLeods have about 25 permanent employees on the farm and hire about 160 others during peach season to operate the packing house and harvest the crop.

The farm grows a variety of row crops in addition to peaches: soybeans, wheat, rye, lespedeza, and corn. Operations are spread out. As Beth says, "Our farm is not all together. We farm in Cheraw. We farm in Birdtown, which is outside of Hartsville in Darlington County. We farm in Lee County over in Bishopville. We farm towards Jefferson, along 151. That's all row crops, but the peaches are everything. And all our peach trees are here in Chesterfield County."

The McLeods have about 400 acres of peach trees. One of their major varieties is the "Cary Mac," discovered and patented by the McLeod family. The farm markets its peaches under the "Mac's Pride" label. Its peach season is a long one, running from late May through late August. The peak season runs from the second or third week in June through the third week of July. The farm enjoyed a good year in 1997, packing about 400,000 half-bushel boxes of peaches.

The farm's retail stand draws a lot of in-season business. Located on Highway 151, a major traffic route to the beaches from Charlotte, the farm designed the new stand to appeal to families when the road was widened two years ago. It has an ice cream parlor, clean, modern bathrooms, and a screened porch. When they built the stand, the family put in a "u-pic-em" strawberry operation right beside it. The 8,000 berries that each acre produced the first year weren't enough ("We'd run out by two o'clock," Beth reports), and they increased the acreage for this year.

The farm shipped more than 4,000 gift packs of peaches through UPS last year. A new station on the line in the packing house is being installed this year to handle the gift packs. New machinery for individual bar-code pricing labels for each peach is also being added to the line.

"We lost three customers last year because we didn't put a sticker on each peach," Beth reports. "Like Kemp says, 'If you're going to run with the big dogs, you can't stay on the porch. You got to get out and run with 'em.'"

The farm was the first in the state to install wind machines in its orchards in 1988 and now has 25 of them. Each machine consists of an 18-foot-long propeller mounted at the top of a 35-foot steel mast. Powered by a 150-horsepower engine, the propeller turns at 600 rotations per minute, circulating the air above the surrounding 15 acres. The machines mix the warmer air above the orchard with the cooler air on the orchard floor and circulate the air in the trees. They are expensive—$15,000 to $20,000 for a single, new unit—but they can save a peach crop, effectively protecting emerging peach buds from killing frosts.

Campbell McLeod, Kemp's father, estimates that the machines can make a "three or four degree" difference, limiting cold damage down to about 25 degrees. But during a severe drop in temperatures, like the one that visited the McLeod farm, Cash Farms, and everyone else in the Southeast in 1996, the machines can't help.

"We lost over half our buds in '96 even before bloom time," he says. "We had two more hard frosts during bloom, and that just wiped us out. We had about a 2-1/2 percent crop that year."

The McLeods now have another machine to combat Mother Nature. Last year they installed three "hail cannons," and, at the moment, they are the only farmers in South Carolina to have them. Although there is considerable debate whether the expensive machines actually deter hail, the family is convinced they are worth the investment. (The French manufacturer that the McLeods talked with was asking $145,000 a unit. The McLeods eventually bought their cannons from New Zealand for about $40,000 each. They cost $150 an hour to run.)

Each hail cannon consists of a large, steel cone set on end, the mouth of the cone open to the sky about 20 feet above the ground. A small shed adjoins the structure.

The cannon "shoots out" noise. Theoretically, the sound waves created and emitted by the devices disrupt the formation of the hail.

As Campbell explains it, the operation of the cannon is simple: "The sound waves go up and break up the hail. Acetylene fuels the cannon. You got these spark plugs in there that set off the gas. The tanks in the shed next to the cannon store the gas. When a storm comes up, you run it, normally for 15 to 20 minutes. We've run it as long as an hour, however long the storm lasts."

"The secret is to be sure to set them off beforehand. With weather forecasts now, we can pretty much pinpoint the storms before they hit. You try to set the cannons off 15 minutes before the hail would arrive. You don't want to wait until the hail comes. You can call it in, set them off by dialing a phone number."

The McLeods think that the cannons work, but their belief is tempered somewhat by the cannons' newness and the difficulty in finite measurement of their effectiveness. Because the McLeods set the cannon off at the approach of storms, before the formation of hail, they don't really know if the hail would have formed or not—with or without the cannon.

Last year, the cannons were set off six or seven times, and the farm received no hail damage—a good beginning. The McLeods will feel more confident about the effectiveness of the devices if the farm continues to escape hail over a period of several seasons.

For now, the McLeods are willing to place their faith in modern technology, and the rest of the state's peach farmers are watching. "Well, we were sort of laughed at when we put in these hail cannons," Campbell says, "but we were laughed at when we put in these wind machines, too."

Beth McLeod and Hail Cannon. McLeod Farms. McBee, South Carolina. February, 1998.

Jerry Gaines. Inman, S.C. July, 1998.

Ned and Woodrow
Potter. Potter Store.
Cowpens, South
Carolina. May, 1997.

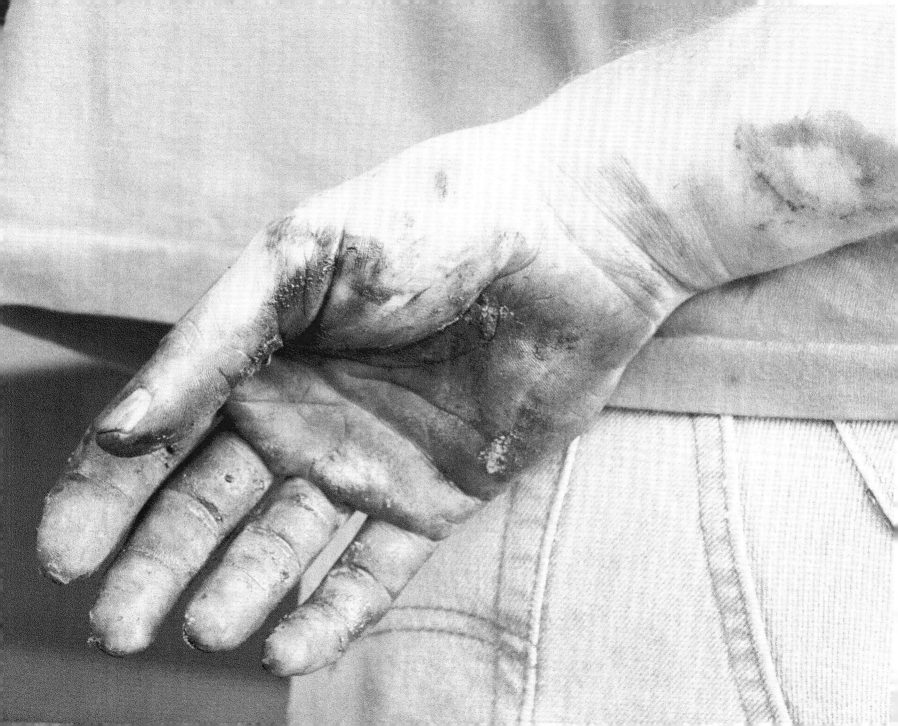

PACKING PEACHES

Monday, June 23, 1997

Today is the first day that the packing house is open and running at Cash Farms. "It's been a long dry spell," Kline says. "I'm ready to get going. I just hope it's going to be enough. It's going to be close. It just all depends on what our volume is, on what our size is, and on what the market does." As he prepares to pack the first harvested fruit of the season, he knows that it is not enough to have grown and gathered the best possible fruit. He has to sell the peaches too.

Keystone Fruit Marketing Inc. in Greencastle, Pennsylvania, has been Cash Farms' broker since 1991. One of their field reps, Mike Mastropietro, is on hand today. Mike's home is in Rochester, New York, and he works all over for Keystone. He was in Georgia earlier last week, working with a Vidalia onion grower. Kline is always glad to see Mike, whom he describes as a "little-bitty, short, bald-headed, Italian Yankee." Mike works hard to try to give the sales force at the home office in Pennsylvania an accurate estimation of what is being packed each week and helps ensure that orders are going out on the right trucks at the right time. His company counts on his experience heavily. If there is trouble with a crop—a shortage—the company needs to know right away so that it can make adjustments with their customers.

Like Kline, Mike is concerned about this year's crop. Looking over the Harvester orchard, Mike worries about the cold damage and the quantity, but thinks, overall, the peaches look pretty good. During his visit to Spartanburg County, he helps scout some nearby orchards belonging to other growers, thinking it might be worthwhile for Cash Farms to try to buy the neighboring crops for packing. It's something Kline has done before. But what Mike looked at was in "pretty poor shape." It looks like all the fruit that Cash Farms will pack this season will be homegrown.

The broker is important to any peach grower who wishes to sell the fruit in quantity outside his area. He makes contracts with vendors and retailers of every description. The growers want him to sell all of the peach harvest for the highest price possible. The broker can make or break the year for a farm. Peaches are a perishable commodity, and prices fluctuate greatly from season to season and even within a single season. Some years, there is an oversupply and prices plummet. Unlike grain farmers, peach growers can't put their product in a silo and wait for the price to go up. The fruit has to be harvested and sold when it is ready. Even farms with sizable refrigerated storage like Cash Farms can only store so many peaches for so long before they run out of room or the fruit goes bad. Now, with the emphasis on picking more mature fruit, it is more important than ever to load the truck and get the product to market as soon as possible.

Cash Farms, like most of the commercial peach growers in the region, wholesales to the "fresh peach" market—grocery stores and produce stands. Growers hope to have a contract for their peaches while they are still on the trees rather than waiting to sell them on the open market at a commodity price.

Years ago, the Washington Street Market in lower Manhattan and others like it in major cities in the East and the Midwest were the centers for the marketing of fresh peaches. Growers would ship their peaches to the big markets by rail and sell them "on the street." Gradually, the system changed. By 1960, trucks had replaced railroads as the primary carrier of the fresh peach crop, and as a result, buyers could get better peaches sooner, shipped directly from the growers.

Growers, like Kline's neighbor Buck Price, found they needed packing sheds. Buck, now 70 years old and retired, opened his packing house along Highway 11 outside of Gaffney in the early sixties.

"We packed with Kline's father before, but we found out right quick that if we wanted to stay in business, we'd have to have our own packing house," he says, sitting at the kitchen table in his Cherokee County home, several miles from Cash Farms. Buck cut every log in his shed himself from locust trees in the mountains not far from here and opened his shed in 1963. He developed his own label, "Big Buck," and for many years used a broker out of Florida.

In 1995, Buck left the peach business after enjoying the best season he ever had. There were plenty of tough years in between. Now he leases his acreage to Kline.

"You can't exist on retailing. Once upon a time, we did have a lot of trucks come in here to buy peaches, but no more. You might sell a few, but today you need to sell 10,000 bushels, and you have to have them sold before you pack them. You can't depend on these truckers. You can't depend on these handle-basket people either. They'll buy 200 bushels and want a price on 1,000, but never show back up or just want 100. You can't live on 100. You have to have the volume."

There was never enough hydro-cooler storage for his peaches either. "You go picking three loads a day, and in 10 days you got something full. They'd keep a week after we packed them, and they'd stay in good shape. We knew what was coming up, hoped to anyway. That was what was so tough at times. You'd make a good crop and get down to your best peaches, and they

wouldn't buy them. The market would just shut off."

The market is cruel to small growers, and two years removed from the business, Buck has strong opinions about what it takes to be successful. "I think if somebody could stay with it now and do the right varieties and do what Kline is doing, he could make it. Kline's shed is modern, he can do that tray-packing. The chain stores want that tray packing—they want those individually packed peaches. I believe a man who is equipped to do that can stay in the peach business.

"I think some people will make it, and I think Kline is one of them. He's a hard worker, and his boy is just out of college and could be somewhere with a better job, but he's over there with his father digging, trying to make it."

Looking over some market reports from New York on his computer in the office, Kline knows that it won't be a very profitable year for Cash Farms. As a matter of fact, "after crunching the numbers, if everything I projected materializes, we'll be back to a break-even situation," he says. "If we did that with the short crop we have, I'll be happy. I'd rather have a big crop, but I'm kind of glad I don't have these early peaches. The prices are in the doghouse. Bad.

Real bad." The 2-1/8 inch peaches are bringing six dollars a box. And that's the price before the grower pays freight and brokerage fees.

Kline isn't the only grower in the region who points to one particular broker "for messin' up the whole deal," overloading the market with a huge volume from a few large growers.

In the past, Cash Farms has had several brokers, including Blue Goose and Seald Sweet out of Florida. One year, Kline even tried to do it himself. "I found out I couldn't do it all myself, run the packing house, try to keep an eye on the field *and* broker. I just about killed myself trying to that year."

From 1980 to 1987, Kline's sister Gwen brokered the farm's peaches. Gwen, who is two years older than Kline, worked on the farm all her life before leaving it in mid-life to start a successful career in real estate. She now runs a prominent local firm's office and has brought her two daughters into the home sales business.

Gwen first began working the packing house "pulling ropes" when she was six years old. That meant she sat up high above the packing line and worked the wooden slats that shuttled the graded peaches from the line to the ring packers. It wasn't a job anyone could daydream on. "Wake up, boy! The peaches are running over!" Woodrow would shout if the young boy that usually worked the ropes was inattentive. Gwen

doesn't remember having to hear, "Wake up, girl!" when she was on the job. She was trying to please her father much too much to fail to do her best.

She grew up working the season in the packing shed, married at 17, and was out in the fields supervising field work by the time she was 19. fifteen years later, she switched over to the office, keeping books and then becoming the farm's broker, selling fruit throughout the Eastern United States, Canada, and Mexico. She was an active member of the Growers' Association and was the first female to be on the program at a national peach convention.

She took over in the field full-time for her father after he suffered his first heart attack in 1963. She remembers her father, still ill, at the dinner table pondering whom he could get to supervise the field work, a job he had done all of his adult life. When she piped up and volunteered, "Why, I can do it, Daddy!" Woodrow turned red in the face and declared that she "wouldn't last two hours out in that sun."

Eventually, Woodrow agreed to allow his daughter to help him (probably because there was no one else, she says) and took her out to the fields to show her how to best nurture the peach trees that were the family's livelihood.

Just 19 and with a two-month-old baby at home, Gwen would begin work at seven in

Ladders. Sunny Slope Farms. April, 1997.

the morning and end at six in the evening with an hour for lunch, the same as everyone else in the field.

"Well, Daddy got nervous and came out to check up on me after a few days," she recalls. "We were thinning, and every peach farmer knows that you don't check the trees by looking at the fruit on the ground—you look at the trees. Even when you know it, you can't help but do it sometimes, and the ground was just covered with little green peaches.

"Daddy looked at the ground this time and put his arm around Tom, an old man that everyone called Uncle Tom and who had worked on the farm since my Daddy was a boy. This was before we used migrant labor. He put his arm around Tom and said, 'Uncle Tom, ain't you taking a little too many off?'

"Well, after that, it took me two weeks to straighten everything out again! These men were used to doing what my Daddy wanted, not this 19-year-old girl. I was mad. I finally told Daddy, 'Daddy, these men won't listen to me if you come out in the field. They'll just do what they want to do, or what they think you want them to do. I can do this job, but you have to leave me alone to do it. You have to quit coming out there.'

"And he did. For the next 15 years, I worked the fields and Daddy only came out twice in those 15 years, both times when I asked him to."

When Gwen came out of the field in 1978, her brother Barry took over. "I left him alone, too," she says. "I didn't go back out there after I came into the office. I knew he didn't need me looking over his shoulder."

She remembers being a little nervous about taking on the job of broker for the farm. She called her longtime friend, Louis Caggiano of Sunny Slope Farms, for his advice. Louis encouraged her to try it.

"You can do it. You just have to just jump into the water," Gwen remembers Louis telling her over the phone.

"Well, what if I start to drown?" Gwen asked.

"Louis just started singing the words to that old hymn, 'Throw Out the Lifeline' to me over the phone. Louis sure couldn't sing a lick, but he was a good friend, and I followed his advice and never regretted it. I've laughed many a time since then, thinking about him and that time."

For the 1997 season, Kline has hired Pam Jones, a friend of his daughter Cindy, to handle the mail orders and promote direct gift-pack sales. The post office has worked with the growers in developing a marketing program over the past few years and provides growers with an attractive box that protects the fruit in shipping. Each box contains 20 peaches and

Louis V. Caggiano, Sr. June, 1997.

Grading Line. June, 1997.

information about the farm. Cash Farms charges $19.95 per box, plus shipping. The post office will deliver the package within two days to any address east of the Mississippi. The business is potentially a very profitable one for the farm and something that Kline has been thinking about for a long time.

In the 1980s, he was preparing to pack and ship for Oregon-based Harry & David, the largest perishable-fruit mail-order outfit in the country. "They visited the farm, picked out an orchard and everything. We contracted to provide all the peaches east of the Mississippi for them. They delivered four truckloads of boxes and packaging materials, and I rented a warehouse to store it all. Two weeks before we were scheduled to start packing for them, I had to call and cancel the deal. The peaches weren't big enough. And I had irrigated that block as much as I could.

"We left the deal in place for the next year, but we got froze out, and they went somewhere else after that.

"I've tried a lot of things, but there are still a few tricks up my sleeves yet. You better believe I'm getting ready to try a few things after this season."

On this day, the first day of packing season, Kline is wondering if he'll get any peaches packed at all. Only 32 of the 50 workers who were contacted by phone on Friday (mostly high school students), have shown up at 8 a.m. Some will arrive later in the morning, and Cindy and Vickie will call around and find others to work in place of those who don't come in. There are 60 bins of peaches in the cooler and more being picked. Chad and an electrician are trying to repair a labeling machine that isn't working. The first truckload of graded and packed peaches is scheduled for Wednesday.

When the line does finally get started, Kline and Chad are all over the place, giving instructions and attending to little kinks in the complex system of machinery, belts, rollers, and bins. The machinery doesn't resemble a finely-tuned assembly line as much as it does a Rube Goldberg-like contraption designed to frustrate and enrage its operator. It's quite noisy, and when the packing house is in operation, the packers lean closely and talk loudly to be heard. All over are buttons and switches to control the supply of current to the dozens of individual motors in this melange of machinery. There are several master switches located in strategic positions that enable the entire line to be shut down at once. This will happen several times this morning, but Kline does not seem to get overly excited.

"The first day is always slow," Kline will later remark, unperturbed by the interruptions.

Chad and Kline have been working on the pack-

Yeah, Baby! Chad Cash.
June, 1997.

ing house off and on all year. They have made several changes in the line and added new machinery. A 50-foot conveyor arrived just last week. This first day of operation also serves as the line's dry run, and Kline treats it as such, patiently stopping the line and clearing clogged spray nozzles, making adjustments on machinery, and closely examining the fruit for undue wear or abrasion by the machinery.

The individual-label machines put a tiny label on each piece of fruit before it goes into the box.

"We started individually labeling in '94," Kline says. "We got the hand-labelers in '94 and these automatic machines in '95. I saw right away that those hand machines weren't going to work out. There were labels everywhere—on kids' foreheads, their ears, the ends of their noses. They'd go around wiping labels on everything and everybody."

Over the years, Kline has paid a lot of attention to the farm's packing house. He is constantly trying to improve it. His goal this year is to sell 90 percent of the fruit that comes out of his orchard. Most growers with packing houses average 75 percent, culling those that aren't up to their standards. The growers who sell to roadside stands and handle-basket merchants sell as much as 98 percent of their crop, Kline says. Some years, though, because of hail and excessive rainfall, Cash Farms has dropped as low as 60 percent.

"That difference—that 30 percent between 60 and 90—that could mean several hundred thousand dollars' difference on my bottom line."

Kline would report later that they ran at 82 percent on this first day. He figures the packing house ran at 80 percent on the second day and at 75 percent the next.

Wednesday, June 25, 1997

The packing house is about to start up again, and the first shipment of fruit will be trucked out today. The Spartanburg newspaper's food section features two peach articles today, one on peach recipes and one about the James Cooley farm and family. The advertising insert for the Harris-Teeter supermarkets is promoting South Carolina peaches at 39 cents a pound (limit 10) as part of a one-day produce sale.

When Mike Mastropietro hears about the sale, he shakes his head. "That's bad. That will drive the prices down."

Bob Smith, a Spartanburg County middle school teacher and part-time peach farm inspector, is here today just as he was on Monday. Bob has been with the U.S. Department of Agriculture inspection service since the mid-seventies when the agriculture department had about 20 inspectors employed in the summers to work at the numerous packing houses then active in the county. Now, he's the only one. He oversees the farms that want to put "USDA-Inspected" stamps on their boxes. Bob periodically pulls a box of peaches off the end of the line and takes a sampling of peaches from the box, inspecting each one for any defects, inserting a thermometer in one to check its core temperature and checking the size with a hand-sizer. If a box is out of grade—if too high a percentage of the peaches have defects—Bob will alert Kline.

The peaches are running well within grade. Kline continues to run the line slowly, and he has a full-time quality control person who works with him keeping a close eye on the grading.

Chad tells a story about one inspector he remembers well. The inspector, whom Chad characterizes "as always being real hyper," had dropped his thermometer through the grate and into the water trough that runs through the floor of the packing house. The trough carries the waste peaches, those deemed too poor for any sale, through the shed and outside to the conveyer pit by the truck docks.

After the inspector dropped his thermometer into the trough, he came to get Chad.

"This guy was real excitable anyway. Now he was real upset, saying, 'What can I do? What can I do?'

"Well, we pulled up the grates where he dropped the thermometer and looked. It was gone. It probably got carried along with the peaches out to the pit. He wanted to search out there—he was really worked up about that thermometer—so we went outside, climbed up, and I took off the grates over the pit to help him look.

"Well, we'd been packing a lot and hadn't cleaned it out for five or six days, and that pit was full of peach scum: leaves, skin, smelly and ripe. A thick, crusty scum had formed over the top of it all.

"I turned around, and whoosh! The next thing I know is this inspector fella was up to his hat in peach slime. He must've thought that it was real shallow or something and stepped off into it to feel for his thermometer. It scared me. I pulled him out. The inspector took off running down there by the docks and around to the front. I laughed a little then, watching him."

The peaches come off the line at several places. The number twos (saleable culls that have minor defects detected by the graders) are put in handle baskets or boxes. The

Sampling. July, 1997.

peaches making grade are sorted by the electronic weigh-sizer, flow out to be individually stamped, and then are loaded according to size in the half-bushel Panta-Paks at several stations. The Panta-Paks separate, hold, and cushion each peach inside the box.

The boxes from each loading station are rolled down to the conveyor belt at the end of the line where they are off-loaded and stacked on wooden pallets. Each stack is about 5-1/2 pallets high, and the loaded pallets are wrapped with heavy tape. After a pallet is loaded and wrapped, a forklift operator lifts it and carries it into storage at the smaller of the packing house's two coolers.

Mike Mastropietro will supervise the season's first shipment of peaches this morning. The operator of the truck is hauling a half-load of tomatoes from downstate, and Mike has the tomatoes off-loaded so that the pallets of peaches can be loaded into the nose of the refrigerated trailer. Then the tomatoes are put back in. The peaches will be going to a market in the Pittsburgh area.

On a break in the office, Kline talks about this year's prospects. "Tough year, this year. Tough all way 'round. Georgia predicted 250 loads a week. The closest they've got is 235. The rest is 165, 175 loads a week. They're about done when they get out of Red Globes. They had low chillin' hours. And some of their late varieties, the high chillers, like Crest Haven, O'Henry, didn't set a good crop anyway. So Georgia, when they get out of Red Globes, they're basically out of peaches.

"Our Harvesters, Red Globes are coming on fast. I been looking at those Staggs over there; they're breaking a little color. They're bad to rot anyway. I got chastised by Buck this morning about his orchard: 'Get those peaches knocked off.' The first day Larry's not picking I'll send him up there."

The Red Globes will be ready in a few days. Mike has bet Kline a cup of cappuccino that they'll get 400 or more bushels an acre out of the Red Globes. Kline doesn't think they'll make that.

Thursday, July 10, 1997

It's early evening, and after a short dinner break, the packing house is running again. The shed has been packing since 9 a.m. and will continue to pack until 9 or so tonight, trying to fill orders. Mike Mastropietro, back in town today after enjoying a good break with his family in New York, reports that things look a little "short" today. There are three truck-loads due to be loaded tonight—two full trail-ers and one partial—and it looks like they will be coming up about 30 percent light.

Mike says it's not Kline's fault; the Keystone salespeople have oversold. It's not the end of the world, but it is not taken lightly either. No-body wants to leave the customer short-handed very often.

Larry's crew finished up the Harvesters last week and started in on the Red Globes.

Unfortunately, it looks like Kline is going to win his coffee wager with Mike over the Red Globes. It doesn't look like they will average close to the 400 bushels an acre that they hoped for.

"That's one bet I wouldn't mind losing," Kline says.

Kline reports that the packing house ran "way out of grade—we did maybe 51 percent" last Sat-urday, the day the first of the Red Globes were packed. A little disgusted, Kline says, "It was mostly cold damage. Splits and softs." But the quality of the peaches that are going into a vari-ety of packages today is excellent. The Red Globe peaches are mostly covered in rich crimson and madder reds with a yellow background. Size is good, too. Most are 2-1/2 inches and up. A siz-able quantity are 2-3/4 inch peaches.

Chad reports that the trees need water, but they put off irrigating, hoping that the predicted storm front this evening will bring the needed rainfall.

Toward the end of the evening run, with the line running smoothly, Kline takes a short break out by the open bay doors on the loading dock. A distant storm is in the west, south of the farm and heading closer. The temperature has dropped, and cool breezes pushing ahead of the storm flow over the loading dock.

Kline leans against a half-loaded palette. It's been a long day. He has a touch of arthritis and professes that his legs "get to him" a little bit after being on concrete all day like today. Relax-ing, he tells a story about an old neighbor, Preacher Sprinkles.

"Preacher Sprinkles was one of the early peach growers around here. He was half preacher and half peach grower. His orchards were down Battleground Road, and he had his own pack-ing house. His son and grandson are still on the land. Those cattle you see in that pasture land along the road belong to them.

"Preacher would be out in the *coldest* weather pruning those trees. He'd say that he couldn't do anything about the weather, but he could do his part and have the trees pruned.

"I remember one time somebody had been in the orchard stealing Preacher's peaches, and someone asked Preacher what he was going to do about it. Preacher said, 'Well, if somebody wants to rob a few bushels of peaches and go to hell, I'll provide the peaches.'

"Back when those tornadoes came through up here in 1973, there was a lot of damage up and down this road. After the storm came through, there were trees and lines down all along through here, and Daddy and I got in the truck and picked our way down the road to look at the damage. When we got up by Preacher's house, it was just covered up in broken trees, limbs, downed power lines, telephone lines—you could hardly see it. Daddy said we'd better stop and check on Preacher. So we carefully picked our way through the yard, stepping over power lines, moving branches and stuff to get to the porch. We could see Preacher and his wife just sitting in the living room, both reading the Bible. When we asked them how they were making out, Preacher declared, 'Just fine, after this little storm has blown over.'"

At one time there were 270 acres of peach trees on the Sprinkles farm off Battleground Road. After the tornado leveled the packing house in 1973, the family pushed up the orchard, and now 100 cattle graze in rolling pasture land. "We didn't leave one tree, got rid of all of them," Preacher's son, Jesse recalls.

Now 77 years old, Jesse remembers "setting out new peach trees with the mule and that big shovel-plow making the furrow and us trying to follow the contour. Later, we'd checkerboard the new trees, you know, making it easier to cultivate and spray." Those first trees cost 15 cents apiece and came from a nursery in Tennessee that supplied most of the growers in the South Carolina Piedmont.

Jesse isn't optimistic about the future of peaches in Spartanburg.

"It comes, and it goes. The peaches left the sandhills of North Carolina years ago, and there is nothing left but a few stumps. Most of the trees around here have been pushed up or abandoned. Peaches are on their way out now. In a few years, there won't be any peaches left in this area.

"Kline is one of the few trying to hang in there, and I don't know if the cost of production is going to run him off. That's what happened to us. Just ate up all of our revenue."

Kline shuts down the line at 9 p.m., and dozens of workers quickly head out to their cars and trucks or to rides waiting for them. The migrant workers will make the short walk down Cash Peach Road to the trailers they're staying in. The storm is closer, and it feels like it's going to wash over the packing house any minute.

Cindy's mother-in-law, Cathy, has cooked dinner for the expanded version of the Cash family that is working late tonight. The packing house's kitchen counter and stove top are crowded with dishes and pans holding the salads, pinto beans and ham, fruit, corn muffins, and rice that Cathy has prepared. Someone else has brought in a peach cobbler. Cathy, Vickie, and her sister, Becky, are eating in Kline's office. Cindy, Celeste, and Pam are having something out in their office. Mike is on the phone in another office. Others come in: Jeff, in his Broad River Electric Co-Op work clothes; his little brother, Nick, bare-chested in overalls, who has been making boxes all evening in the packing house loft; Clay, on a break from the forklift. They wash up, fill a plate, laugh, talk, and find a seat. When there are no more chairs, some lean against a wall or cabinet.

Kline comes in to wash up and has some supper before doing his paperwork. Chad and a small group are loading the last boxes packed today onto palettes. They will break for dinner after they get the peaches into cold storage and go back to load two more trucks due later tonight.

The storm that passes through Spartanburg and Cherokee counties is fierce. The weather bureau will report that some areas received as much as six inches of rain from it. South of Battleground Road toward Spartanburg, the water overflows the ditches, and much of the roadway is under water for a brief time.

Most of the storm misses Cash Farms. Kline will find less than two-tenths of an inch of water in the rain gauge the next morning.

North past the Sprinkles farm on Battleground Road, less than a quarter mile after turning west onto Highway 11 toward Chesnee, is the Hatchette peach shed, set back off the highway. More than 10 years have passed since peaches ran through this packing house. On a hot August day, Ruth Scruggs Hatchette McBrayer decides to open it up. Ruth McBrayer, known around here as "Miss Hatchette," is 85 years old and spent a good portion of her life running this shed.

The fields around the shed were once covered in Dixie Gems, Red Havens, Early Red Frees, Elbertas, and Rangers. Her late husband, Gene Hatchette, bought land here, adjacent to his father's peach farm, during World War II. Two years later, Gene and his two brothers built this shed. Ruth was 33 when the packing house be-

Hatchette's Peach Shed. December, 1996.

gan operating.

"I helped some but didn't think I really was part of that operation until, one day, I had come home from lunch and was late coming back for some reason. When I got to the shed, the shed wasn't running, and it was already past time. When I asked Gene why it wasn't running, he said, 'Why, we were waiting for you!' That's when I began to realize that I was somewhat important to the business."

In 1944, Gene's father died, and then Gene died suddenly in 1947, leaving Ruth in charge.

"We ran the shed in '47 after Gene died. In 1946, I had told Gene—now, these were my words and you're going to think I'm awful, but I said them: 'Now, I know how to do everything in this packing house except set those machines (the sizers), and I'll be *damned* if I'll learn to set those things!'" She laughs now when she remembers making that stand. "Later, when I was setting those machines all those years, I would always think of those words."

As she walks toward the shed, she passes a small abandoned house, windows broken and open to the weather.

"That house was built in 1865 by my uncle, Memory Scruggs," she says. "We always had people in it for as long as I can remember, but we haven't had anyone in there for a long time now.

"The trees that Gene had planted had come into their prime when Gene died—they were at their very best. People gave me a lot of credit for doing 'such a wonderful job,' but I really didn't deserve it because the trees that Gene had planted were there. I bought other land after Gene died and put in more peaches. At one time, we had about 200 acres, and we had tenants and farmed cotton, corn, hay, I don't know what all, but after Gene's death, I really didn't farm but for the peaches.

"My heart was in the peaches. It was my life. These peaches, this orchard became my life. I just absolutely lived it. I worked. I worked all the time. I went to the peach meetings. I listened to all the peach lectures. I studied the peach books. I really tried to educate myself. I realized if I was going to do this job, I needed to learn how to do it."

Outside the packing house, there are a few peach trees still standing. They've gone wild now and are overgrown with weeds.

"Those trees I have left aren't any good. They're gone. I had a good Loring field, but they don't hardly bloom anymore. I don't do anything with my land. I could sell it at a high price, but I guess I'll let somebody else deal with it. I haven't got rid of any of it. I pay taxes it on it mostly.

"Kline Cash leased some of it last year and this year. He is trying to keep from going under. I

Packing. June, 1996.

admire him for it. I hope he will do well this year. If he could have one real, real good year, that would save him, I think."

Ruth remarried in 1969. In the early eighties, her husband, Charles McBrayer, advised her to quit packing peaches. But she and her niece, Faye, kept it going until 1985.

"Finally, I made my mind up not to pack one year. I didn't prune. Didn't spray. And when they got froze out next year, I was so glad. I was so glad, because to see those peaches on those trees, and nobody looking after them would have broken my heart."

The peach shed, though abandoned except for storage, is still painted white (the way Ruth always insisted), and the glare off the boards is intense. After the padlock is removed, a sizeable door is shoved sideways until there is an opening wide enough to walk through into the shed.

The old wooden grading line is still in place on the dirt floor, bare bulbs dangling from their cords above it. The old hydro-cooler, which would sometimes use two and three truckloads of ice a day, is off to one side. Two old rusty tractors have been driven or pushed into storage on sections of the shed floor. Hoses, belts, and wires hang in loops from the walls and rafters. One whole side of the floor is covered with stacks of old wooden orchard bushel boxes and the big wooden field bins. A sign hanging by wire from the rafters admonishes: "Please Do Not Eat Peaches In The Shed." On one wall, near the office in one corner, is a Pepsi-Cola chalkboard.

"Thieves broke into the office one year after we closed this up," Ruth says. "Stole a beautiful old antique desk in there and just dumped everything out on the floor. Made a mess of everything."

Old galvanized picking buckets hang in bunches by their canvas straps on the wall by the stairs going up to the loft. The air in the loft, directly beneath the metal roof, is suffocating. It must be 10, 20 degrees hotter than on the shed floor. Anyone up here for long would not envy the "box boys" on a day like this, big fans going or not.

The loft runs the length and width of the shed. Most of this space is relatively uncluttered, unlike the floor below, where Ruth has to edge sideways through a maze of stored goods. Along the long walls beneath the sloping roofline, there are stacks and stacks of unmade flats of corrugated boxes and lids. Some have fallen over. Some of the box lids display Ruth McBrayer's old brand: "Hatchette's Peaches" with a hatchet and a peach limb printed on each one.

Outside, after setting the door back in place and securing the padlock, Ruth brushes herself off and gets back in the car. As she settles in her seat, she looks out at the big white shed, sighs

Walt Posey. October, 1996.

and says, "You know, if I wrote a book about this place, I'd have to call it 'Too Many Memories.'"

Tuesday, July 15, 1997

Brent Belue, a great-grandson of Aunt Vada, and Pam are finishing up loading Vickie's Jeep Cherokee with 40 gift packs of peaches. Pam will take them into Cowpens to mail them this morning.

"These packs make me nervous," Kline says, "but I've only had two complaints so far. I'll send them another package of peaches or refund their money, either one."

Mid-July is normally the height of the season, but the packing house isn't running today. So far this year, the packing house has been closed more often than not. Vickie says that they're scheduled to run a full day Thursday or Friday.

"It's been thin picking this season. We didn't get nearly as much out of the Red Globes as we hoped for. The Red Globes were full of soft tips and split pits; that comes from cold damage. The Blakes are due next, and I sure hope they do better than the Red Globes. I won't say we'll pick 200 acres, I'll say we'll 'walk through' 200 acres of peaches this year.

"Everybody is like that. One day last week there was just eight truckloads of peaches from South Carolina, five from Georgia to leave the state. Most years, one or two packing houses would do that."

Dick Carson and Walt Posey, the mechanic at Cash Farms, are on tractors out in the fields spraying the peach trees. In spring and summer, it is one of their main jobs. At times, they've been spraying every day of the week when it hasn't been raining.

Walt Posey is lucky to be alive. He survived being flipped off the back of a tractor while bush-hogging a peach orchard one day in June 1995. He landed headfirst between the tractor and the bush-hog, his head barely missing striking the machinery. Somehow, he grabbed and held onto a pair of one-inch hoses. The turbo-charged tractor roared through the orchard in third gear, dragging Walt and the trailing bush-hog over two fully mature peach trees, throwing out "stumps as big as five-gallon buckets," before the tractor, slowed by the trees, finally stalled out.

Bloodied by numerous cuts and scrapes, with a deadened arm and a wrecked knee (doctors would later diagnose bone chips in the left elbow and torn cartilage in the knee), Walt was irritated to discover that he had lost his watch.

"It was a real good one, too. I had seen it at J.C. Penney for $69.95 and told myself, 'I'm gonna get me that watch.' And I watched for it to go on sale. When I saw it come down to $49,

I bought it."

Two men were in the orchard and witnessed the accident. They ran to Walt's aid and "had goose bumps so big you could see them across the road, I'd scared them so bad," says Walt, laughing. Walt fussed about his watch, and all three men hunted for it before Walt agreed to be taken to the hospital.

"I never did find it, and I came back plenty of times later to look too."

It wasn't the first time Walt had lost a watch on the farm. "About five, six years ago, I lost a real good one from Sears. It was a $50 one. It had a real big face and a thing that was military time and everything. I got that one on sale too."

Walt points to the hard-packed, red dirt apron on the field side of the garage. "I was working under a truck right here, and the blame thing rolled right over my arm and just crushed that watch." He rolls up the left sleeve of his shirt and taps his forearm. "I had dang treadmarks here on my arm! Pieces of gravel was all in my skin. No bones were broke, but it sure ruint that watch."

Walt was 13 when he quit school and began working at Cash Farms. "I had to go to work. Got tired of being hungry. I had my brother and sister under me, and we all had to eat. Wasn't much, but we ate. We all growed big."

When the March freeze killed the peach crop in 1996, one of the first things that Kline did was lay off all the farm's salaried non-family employees—all except for Walt. He'd been there 40 years.

Today, Walt's arm is bare. When someone asks, "What time is it now, Walt?" he smiles, unbuttons the flap on one of his shirt's chest pockets, and pulls out an inexpensive, plastic black-banded watch.

"Nineteen-ninety-five from K-Mart," Walt says and laughs. "One of my sons gave me a nice watch for Christmas, but I keep it at the house when I'm workin'. When I'm over here now, I just carry this. Keep it in my pocket too."

Thursday, July 31, 1997

The shed ran from 1 to 4 p.m. today, packing 55 bins of peaches. Out in the field, Larry's crew has picked 35 more. Kline reports that they have a load scheduled tomorrow that is destined for Canada. He hasn't had a Canadian load for a while.

Heading back to the big cooler from the office, Kline walks around the packing line, going the long way instead of cutting through. He says sheepishly, "The arthritis in my knees—that left knee, especially—has been getting bad. I paid over a hundred dollars for special insoles—they made casts of the bottom of my feet—but that concrete is still getting to me."

In the cooler, one wall is full of packed peaches. "This is the most peaches I've seen in here in two years," he says.

In a good year, this cooler would be filled with bins. The second, smaller cooler, which has been empty most of this season, would be full of pallets of packed peaches, and the trucks would be pulling in and out of the docks off Cash Farms Road.

The crew is into the Blakes now, an orchard of 20-year-old trees. The farm will finish up the season in August with the Stagg block on the Gossett farm, trees that are 16 years old, and the 17-year-old Rio Osa Gems and Encore orchards.

It's the hottest part of the summer here at Cash Farms, with temperatures regularly in the mid- to high-nineties. Despite the heat, the crew in the orchard wears long sleeves and long pants to protect their skin. Their clothes are soaked through with sweat, and they wear wet towels around their necks. Even in the evenings, it can be 90-plus degrees. Jack Brannon drops by the farm, usually just before sunset, to fill his pickup with Cash peaches to sell the next day in the Asheville, North Carolina, market. He has worked on peach farms in the area all his life,

from picking to pruning to running a crew. He did his first work at Cash Farms 50 years ago. Now age 70, Jack walks with a pronounced limp. He's had problems with his legs since he was a child and has an artificial hip. Chad or Brent or Clay bring out pallets on evenings like this and help him load the bed of his pickup truck with baskets of peaches, stacking them five tiers high.

Jack has seen some hot days in his years in the peach orchards.

"During the hot times, there wasn't much you could do to keep cool except wait for winter," he says, leaning against his truck. "Standing under a peach tree was just as bad as under the sun. Sometimes I was running as many as six different crews picking in different fields, and I'd have to run around all the time checking with them. Now some folks wanted that air conditioning in the truck. Man, I think that was the worst idea you could have. You were always in and out of that truck. With air conditioning, you left that truck, and it seemed like you were hotter then than if you hadn't had it at all.

"When I was growing up, plowing behind the mule, we didn't seem to think about the heat like now. We just didn't pay as much attention to it, I guess."

Jack, tall and fit-looking, was born in 1927 in an area near here known as the "Cowpens Funnies." His family sharecropped, growing their own vegetables and raising cows, hogs, and chickens. "When we was farmin', we didn't have to buy anything hardly except sugar and coffee. Anything we needed, we growed it. We had to. We couldn't have made it otherwise."

Some nights after loading up, Jack drives straight to Asheville and sleeps in his truck so that he's ready to sell peaches when the market opens in the morning. "I hate to do that anymore, though. I'm just getting too stiff for that. That last time, I couldn't hardly sleep any." The alternative isn't much better: "Can't hardly make any money if I pay for a motel. They're high."

He has worked for almost every peach farm in this area. Some of them have changed hands several times in his lifetime.

"I started up at B and G and worked there until they got bought up by the Belues. I've outlived the peaches on that farm. They don't do much peaches anymore. All the sheds are mostly closed around here now. Kline's just about the only one that has a shed open. I think they have maybe one or two in Inman—Gramling Brothers is one of them. Worked for them too. Pruned their trees and picked them."

Not only are the peaches disappearing, so are the people who used to pick them. Crews are hard to find, and some of the pickers don't do a very good job, he says.

"Hands, man, you can't put nothin' on that.

You find some good ones and some bad. You try to get things done for the man you're working for and try to get them done right, and people are doing any kinds of way in picking peaches—they're trying to make that dollar fast: fill up that box. And they're picking peaches you can't run through the shed. It's a lot of aggravation. You got to be out there with them. It's a headache is what it is.

"It used to be, in picking time, I could take the truck to town, and I'd have to stop 'em from getting on the truck. Now you have to beg 'em to get on, and you still won't have nobody. It's just the way it is. I'm thinking—I might be wrong—but I'm thinking that it all comes from the government helping people that's really able to work. There is a lot of people out there getting help who really don't need it. What they need is a job. Work, and get your living. There's so many people who think the world owes them a living."

In his 50 years around the peach business, he has watched many a grower just give up. The overheads are high and the margins low. He's hopeful about the future of Cash Farms, though.

"I think Cash can make it. Kline is a hard-working man, and he believes in the Lord. He don't trust in just hisself. He do what he thinks he need to do and leaves the rest of it to Him. And as long as he does that, Mister, he'll live.

Jack Brannon. July, 1996.

Handle Baskets. June, 1998.   Handle Baskets. July, 1998.

"All that Kline has wanted to do is farm. I knew him since he was born. I knew his father, Woodrow, and his wife, Marie, and seen him and Gwen and them grow up. I seen Walt over there grow up. If anybody will make it, Kline will. He's determined to make it. He's got his son to help him. You don't catch many young boys gettin' out there and doin' like Chad. You can't hardly find a young man to get out there and farm and stick with it like he is doing."

Saturday, September 13, 1997

The season is over. The packing house shut down August 21st, and the final truck of peaches went out on the 29th.

"It turned out much worse than I had hoped for," Kline says, sitting at his desk in the farm office. "Going in, we were looking at a potential of 200,000 boxes. We didn't do but 25,000 or 30,000." He is obviously disappointed but not moaning about it. He has known what the results would be for awhile.

"After that freeze, I knew we'd lost the early and late crop, but I still thought we had a good chance to make maybe a 50 percent crop, something like that. You could tell when we got into the Red Globes, there was a lot more damage than we first thought. The Harvesters turned out to be our highest yield. It was downhill after that."

Sunny Slope Farms picked about 400 acres of peaches, less than one-third of what they used to pick during the farm's heyday. It was enough to run their packing house through the season, though. The Gramlings' packing house didn't pack nearly as many peaches as they had hoped for, but the Johnson brothers reported that they had missed most of the freeze and had a good crop.

Statewide, the industry packed 160 million pounds of peaches, not a banner year, but far better than the 8 million produced in 1996 when the freeze destroyed almost all the crop.

Chad had planned a vacation in Cancun at the end of the season but never made it. "Nah, I wound up going to Myrtle Beach for a long weekend," he says smiling.

Kline spent two days last week in industry meetings in Columbia.

"Clemson came up with this idea of having a 'Vision Team,' and I got put on it. We have to figure out the fruit industry in the Southeast and what Clemson can do to support the growers. Probably, what we are going to wind up doing is do all the research on a regional basis. Clemson, University of Georgia, the USDA station in Byron, Georgia, and N.C. State need to combine their efforts. There's no use duplicating all of their efforts. We need to get some kind of cohesive effort between all of them. Basically, that's what we came up with."

While he was in Columbia, Kline attended a meeting of the Peach Council, and he reports that all the commercial growers in South Carolina but three were there.

"The main topics of conversation were 'How to improve markets,' 'What are we doing wrong?'—the same things we've been hashing out the last 20 years."

Kline always has been active in working to protect and promote his industry. He was one of the leading growers in the founding of the South Carolina Peach Board, has been an elected leader of the National Peach Council, and was the South Carolina Council's president in the past.

At the behest of the state's agricultural department, he traveled to Charlotte and Atlanta last year to help promote South Carolina peaches at regional and international food expos. (Kline was amused that the Charlotte expo had booths from South Carolina's emu and ostrich associations promoting their birds as dining fare. "They were kind of competing against one another. They had samples there. Would cook it right on the spot, you know, and I tried both. They don't taste at all alike.")

He also has been involved in a frustrating series of meetings about proposed changes to the federal crop insurance policy. He has been to meetings in Georgia and Columbia and twice to Washington, D.C., where they met in U.S. Senator Strom Thurmond's office.

Kline realizes the importance of this kind of work. Above all, he is pragmatic. As a farmer he knows he must also be a promoter, a salesman, and a politician. They are roles he is now practiced at, but ones that he does not relish playing.

"I'd much rather be on the seat of a tractor than do this stuff," he says. Spreading his hands and smiling wistfully, he muses, "Sometimes, it seems that I do everything but farm. Things have gotten so complicated around here that I just have to delegate. We couldn't operate this place if I didn't."

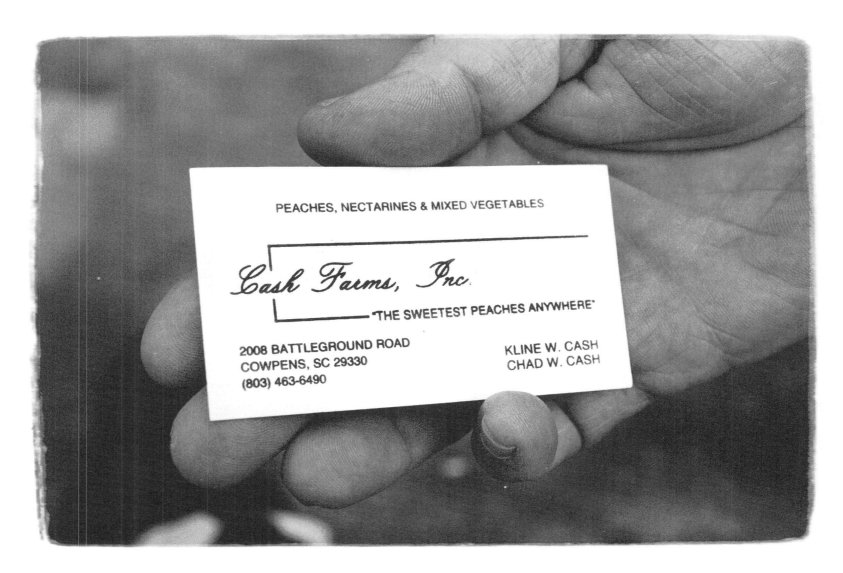

Kline Cash. July, 1997.

DIVERSIFICATION 4

Monday, October 24, 1997

The fields at Cash Farms are awash in white dots. It's time to pick cotton, and Kline is one of the few farmers in the Piedmont growing it. In fact, he's the only farmer who has grown cotton commercially in Spartanburg County since 1984.

Kline's second-hand cotton-picker is working the field, raising a cloud of fine dust that drifts behind in the air before settling to the earth. The Cash farm is returning to its roots—cotton production—in an effort to keep peaches going for another year.

A century ago, the gentle, rolling hills of the Piedmont were covered in cotton, feeding the textile mills that were popping up on nearly every bend of every river. The sharecropping and tenant systems of farming accompanied the first large-scale cultivation of cotton in Spartanburg County, shortly after the Civil War, and by 1880 there were 55,000 acres under cultivation, according to "Hammond's Handbook," a survey written for the USDA by Harry Hammond. That year, Hammond also reported the first widespread use of commercial fertilizer, which enabled Upcountry farmers to compete in production with the old cotton-producing counties of the coastal plain.

During the next 40 years, the farming of cotton intensified in the county. In 1920, Spartanburg led all 46 counties in the state in both bales produced and the value of the crop. At the advent of the Great Depression, cotton production in the county peaked with 135,000 acres in cultivation.

Cotton, however, was an economy that wouldn't last. The Piedmont, with its 50 inches of annual rainfall, its hills, and its thin topsoil, was especially vulnerable to soil erosion.

A 1936 USDA survey of Spartanburg County revealed that erosion "has seriously affected most of the agricultural land . . . with between twenty-five and seventy-five percent of the topsoil removed from at least three-fourths of the county." Many farmers had over-cultivated their land, not resting the soil or rotating the crops. Ever-increasing amounts of fertilizer had been used to enrich the depleted soil. Large amounts of herbicides and insecticides had also been used. Exhausted land was sometimes abandoned and left bare.

By the 1950s, cotton had ceased to be a major crop in the South Carolina Piedmont. The combined production of cotton in the Upstate counties of Anderson, Greenville, and Spartanburg declined from 150,000 acres in 1945 to 12,000 acres in 1970 to 1,500 acres in 1982. By the time Kline Cash put together 200 acres and planted

cotton for the first time in 1996, cotton fields had become a curiosity in the area.

After the bolls opened up in Kline's fields, it wasn't uncommon to see cars slow down or pull over and stop and look. One afternoon as Kline was hooking up a loaded cotton wagon to his truck, a car pulled over and a young woman hopped out, went over to Kline, and excitedly asked him if he'd sell her a branch of cotton for a dollar. It tickled Kline. He accepted her dollar, told her to take what she wanted, and waved to her as she got back in her car with the branch and sped down the road.

"We get a lot of folks that stop by. The old-timers, especially, around here tell of memories of the cotton, and they all have their own stories about picking."

One year ago, on a day just like this, Kline and Chad were working to repair the cotton picker, a 15-year-old John Deere model they had bought from a mechanic in Orangeburg for $15,000. They needed to get it up and running to get the cotton out of the fields—the first cotton grown on this farm since Kline's father planted it in the 1940s.

"If there was one day I could go out and work in the field without some piece of equipment breaking down I'd be real happy," Kline declared that day with a smile and a laugh. Although they had missed some good picking weather, Kline didn't seem unduly worried. Unlike peaches, cotton won't ripen and waste if it isn't picked right away. "One farmer I talked to says there's been years he hasn't finished his cotton 'til right before Christmas."

On that beautiful fall afternoon, Walt Posey was inside the garage rebuilding a tractor. Garrett, home from school, busily scampered about, asking questions, fetching tools, climbing into the picker's cab and atop it, looking out over the bin. Wiping the grease from his hands, Kline spread his arms out and said, "You know the only reason we're doing all this is to be able to keep on growing peaches."

The farm has done a lot of things over the years "to keep on growing peaches." Diversification—what Jack Brannon talks about as "not putting your eggs all in one basket"—is nothing new to Kline. Over the years, the farm has undertaken numerous enterprises to supplement the peach crop. Besides cotton, Kline farmed soybeans, corn, wheat, and strawberries in 1996. This year, he has increased his wheat and soybean acreage and cut back on the cotton acreage.

The farm's small strawberry operation, now in its eighth season, did well this year. A little more than four acres, the berry patch is on a triangle of land formed by Battleground, Double Branch, and Sellars roads. Mostly a "u-pic-em" operation, the strawberries draw a lot of customers to the farm's produce store during April, May, and June. Many customers come back in the summer when the peaches come in.

"The third year, I started makin' a little money," Kline says. "You don't make but a few thousand dollars in a good year—you know, net profit—but it's something I enjoy doing. It gets our peach customers started in early. It's just a little activity in the spring of the year. Gets your adrenalin going."

The old cotton-picker Kline bought last year is still in operation, picking two rows at a time, but he would love to have a four-row picker to save time picking his crop. He knows he can't buy a new one (they run about $150,000), but he is already thinking of scouting around for a used one for next year if he can find the acreage to lease and increase his planting to justify the expense of a decent four- or five-year-old machine.

Dick Carson, who often runs a tractor on the farm, thinks that Kline should have bought a new cotton-picker instead of the used one, which constantly breaks down.

"Lord, Dick, do you know how much one of

Irrigation Pipes. July, 1996.

Cornfield, Irrigation. July, 1996.

Dick Carson. October, 1996.

those costs?" Kline asks.

Dick smiles and replies, "Man, if you're going to go broke, go broke!"

When asked if the 1982 picker came with a warranty, Kline laughs and declares, "When you buy a piece of equipment this old, you get what my brother Barry calls the 'Arkansas Guarantee.' When it breaks in half, you own both halves."

The cage, or basket, of the picker holds about two field bales, or 3,000 pounds of cotton, cottonseed, and trash. When full, the picker is moved alongside a cotton wagon. Hydraulically powered, the picker's basket is then tipped and its load dumped into the wagon. The wagons are simple flatbed trailers enclosed on all sides with eight-foot-high reinforced steel mesh walls.

The picker returns to harvesting the rows until the wagon is full. Kline has two wagons in the field. The larger one is 40 feet long and will hold the equivalent of about 12 bales of cotton. The smaller one holds about eight bales. The cotton gin provides the wagons.

When a wagon is full, Kline or Chad will hook it up to their old '74 Ford dumptruck and haul it to the nearest cotton gin, located in Boiling Springs, North Carolina. It's about a 40-minute trip each way. The next closest working gin is over in York County. The cotton gins that once dotted the landscape in Spartanburg and Cherokee counties have long since gone out of business.

After delivery, the field cotton will be ginned and pressed into 500-pound bales. Cash Farms will pay the gin operator a fee for the ginning.

"Usually, the sale of the cotton seed about covers the ginning cost," Kline says.

Cash Farms can sell the baled cotton to a broker or sell it themselves. The cotton can be stored for later sale or sold immediately. When Kline first planted cotton a year and a half ago, it had been selling for 78 cents a pound. Last year's crop sold for about 71 cents, but the price is going lower than that this year.

"If I didn't need the cash flow—and I really do need the cash flow right now—I'd probably haul it back here and store it in one of the coolers until the price went up. Right now, when everybody is picking, that's when the price is lowest. Everybody wants to sell now, so it's a buyers' market."

Chad says there are some advantages to cotton farming. "As far as cotton, it's not too bad, because you don't have many people to deal with. Peaches, you have a lot of people to deal with, and that's the hardest part about it. Tryin' to get them to do what you need them to do, tryin' to be fair with them and them fair with you. You got about 40 or 50 pickers and 50 or 60 people in the packing house. That's a lot of people to manage."

Chad Cash, Cotton Picker.
December, 1996.

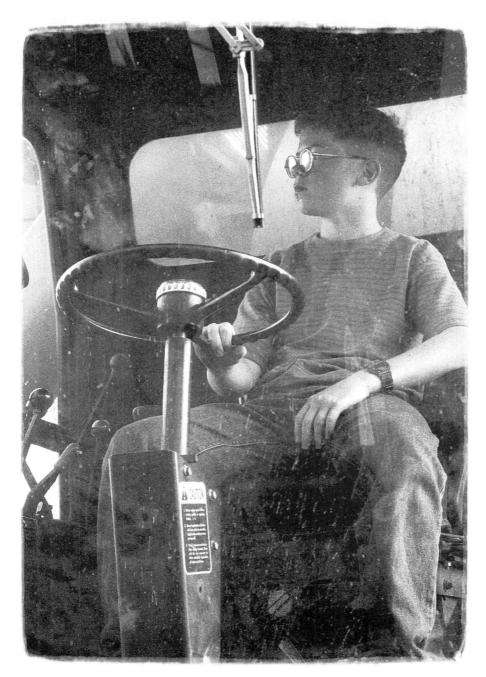

Garrett Cash, Cotton Picker.
November, 1996.

One Friday during cotton-picking season in November 1996, Vickie and Kline went to the nearby town of Chesnee for lunch at Turner's Restaurant and brought back some food for Chad who had spent the morning running the picker. When carrying it into the office, Vickie managed to spill some mashed potatoes and gravy on her dress. Knowing she and Kline had an appointment with their accountant in Spartanburg in the afternoon, Vickie told Kline that she was headed home to change clothes.

Kline, dressed in well-worn, but not-too-dirty khakis and flannel shirt, said, "Okay, I'll be ready when you are."

Vickie looked at him. "In other words, you're not going to change clothes?"

"No, I'm not going to change clothes," he said, amused. "I ain't ashamed, if you ain't."

After Vickie made a face and left the room, Kline called after her, "Now, if you are ashamed to go with me in my dirty clothes, I'll go home and change."

Chad, who had cleaned up the worst of the grease from the picker, was at a desk with his lunch. He was sitting there with grease streaked in his brown hair.

"I know I wash it three or four times at night to get it out. I don't think I've worked on anything nastier than that cotton-picker."

"It still beats workin' cattle," Kline said.

Quickly, Chad replied, "I like workin' cattle better than I do this."

"At least it's not like manure," Kline said. "In the spring of the year, the manure is real thin, and the cattle slap you across the face with those nasty tails. Whew!

"Now Daddy ran probably about a hundred head of pigs when I was real, real little. We used to sneak out in the pasture when the sows was comin' in. We'd grab a little piglet and run, climb up a tree, and squeeze it. That old sow would go crazy and try to tear that tree down. She'd killed us if she ever knocked us out of that tree. Daddy and Momma would of had a fit if they'd known.

"When I was about 12, we was always bad about riding the cows. My daddy, Woodrow, was off to auction at Charlotte—he'd always go one Friday a month—and Barry, Mike Belue, and I would sneak into the cattle barn and ride the cows. One time, we were in there and Mike had jumped on the back of a cow. That cow was leaping and running. At the top of a leap, that cow ran slap into one of those heavy two-by-ten rafters, smacked Mike right square in the forehead, knocked him right off that cow. I thought it had killed him. It did knock him unconscious. Scared us to death.

"The day I decided to get out of the cattle business, we was packing peaches. I think this was in '91. Everything was going crazy. I looked out, and my whole herd was going up the highway. I mean every one of them. I'm trying to pack peaches. No one around to go get them. I said, 'That's it. We're gettin' out of the cattle business.' Cows and peaches just don't mix."

On the bulletin board on the wall behind Kline's desk is a simple map of the United States with all the sizeable seaports prominently noted. Kline put the map up there to remind him about the seaports and an onion import deal that he and his broker, Keystone, have been trying to put together for two years. Keystone is a big importer of Vidalia-type sweet onions from South America in the winter. They have a distribution plant in New Jersey and have been trying to work out a plan that would create another distribution point for the Southeast at Cash Farms.

"I've been trying a long time, trying for years, exploring different things to do with this building in the wintertime," Kline says. "We got such a tremendous investment here, and it just sits here nine, 10 months out of the year doing nothing. I knew there had to be something we could do with it."

Cash Farms was all ready to receive the onions in December 1996, but a transportation problem developed. At the last minute, Keystone could not arrange for trucks to pick up the onions in Cowpens. In the winter, the tiny South Carolina town is off the main produce trucking routes, and the freight costs simply would have been too expensive.

Kline is hopeful that the problem can be overcome this year. If he can make it work, the onions will arrive in containers at the Charleston port in December and be trucked up Interstate 26 to Cash Farms. The crew at Cash Farms will inspect, grade, and repackage them, palletize the boxes, and load them on trucks to be distributed to stores and markets all over the Southeast. The deal will be a big boost for the farm. The conversion needed to switch over from peaches to the packing and inspection requirements for the onions is minimal. Kline and the farm certainly would welcome a reliable source of additional revenue.

There have been other attempts at diversification in the past. Last year, Kline opened the packing house in September to pack something he hadn't packed for many years: apples. An agent in North Carolina worked out a deal between an apple grower in Reidville and some buyers in Virginia and Ohio and, for a

Chad Cash. November, 1996.

Spindles, Cotton Picker.
November, 1996.

few weeks before the northern apple crop came in, Cash Farms was sorting and re-packing Granny Smiths for candy apples, juice, and baby food. Kline says he would do it again if given the opportunity.

In the 1970s, the farm ran its own trucking firm as a sideline, as did several Piedmont peach growers. Kline remembers that it seemed like he spent every weekend working on trucks. They finally got out of it when Barry, Gwen, and Kline finally convinced Woodrow that they were losing money on the deal.

For nearly 20 years, the Cashes sold fertilizer from a plant in Spartanburg, but that business ceased to be profitable too. "We hauled thousands and thousands of tons of fertilizer," Kline says. "Me and Barry and Walt spread that fertilizer all over Spartanburg, Cherokee, and Union counties and north up in North Carolina. We were probably the biggest distributor of fertilizer up here for several years. We had three tractor spreaders, three truck spreaders, two Killebrews, one or two flatbeds, and three tractor-trailers, and we couldn't keep up in the spring of the year.

"We got out of it in the early eighties when soybeans went to $4, cows were cheap, and interest rates went to 20 percent, and everybody quit farmin'."

Then there were the years when Cash Farms ran a grain elevator.

"We ran it four or five years, then, again, the soybean prices went to $4, interest rates shot up, and everybody got out of the row-crop business. We just shut it down. We wound up selling it at auction."

One of Kline's strengths is this willingness to try new things, to stretch, and to take risks. Right now, his biggest disadvantages are his size and the uncertainty of the peach crop from year to year. Just maintaining what he's got, let alone expanding, is awfully tough when every year is a crapshoot.

Overall, Kline is philosophical about the livelihood he and seven generations of the Cash family have chosen.

"Farming is just like any other business. There's companies that go out of business every day, nobody cries over it. Why should anybody cry over a farm going out of business? There is a lot of truth to that. Sure, it is a way of life, but, still, it is a viable business. You got to look at it like a business, and if you are not making a profit doing one thing, you better quit and do something else. What I've always tried to do is try something and if it doesn't work, go on to something else."

J.D. and Garrett, Cotton Wagon. November, 1996.

EPILOGUE

Wednesday, April 22, 1998

It has been an eventful winter for Cash Farms.

The onion deal with Keystone fell through again. Chad had made two trips to New Jersey to work on the deal. Equipment needed for the onion grading and packaging had been located and was on order. Keystone finally secured the freight rate needed to make the whole thing work. Everything, it seemed, was in place. Kline was expecting his first load in December when he got the bad news: No onions. Before the El Nîno rains arrived, parts of Peru suffered a drought, and the onions just shriveled in the field. Keystone says the offer still stands for next year, and Kline is hopeful.

In early fall, Cindy took a temporary job at an office in Inman and kept it until February.

During December, Kline turned the back end of the packing house into a warehouse for a paper recycling plant in Cowpens, storing pallets of compacted, corrugated cardboard. The plant was stocking up on raw materials through the holiday season, and Kline was making a few dollars off-loading it from trailers and warehousing it for a few weeks.

In December, Gwen was named "Realtor of the Year" among the hundreds of real estate agents in Spartanburg County.

Walt Posey was laid off for several weeks in late fall. He continued to work in the farm's garage, repairing lawn mowers and automobiles for people in the area.

Most of the field crew continued to live in the camps along Cash Peach Road and did work where they could find it.

Kline canceled the farm's order for 10,000 new Contender trees for this year. "I told Phillip there was no sense buying what I couldn't pay for. It will be all right. I have the rest of my life to plant trees."

Kline and Vickie made it to the growers' convention in Savannah in January.

After a mild winter with just one small snowfall, three nights of subfreezing temperatures hit the Upstate in March. On three successive nights, March 10-12, the temperature at Cash Farms fell to 18 degrees.

Amazingly, most of the peaches at Cash Farms survived. Orchards elsewhere in the state that had "bloomed out" were lost. "If this had been a week or 10 days later, it would have cleaned us out," Kline says.

Kline's happiness over his narrow escape is tempered by his knowledge of others who were not as fortunate.

"I talked to Kemp McLeod. He said he hasn't checked everything yet, but he may have suffered 50 percent damage. Georgia was supposed to have been hit really bad. Some of the counties have already been designated disaster areas."

During those three subfreezing nights, Kline and Chad alternated nights irrigating the strawberries because a coat of ice will actually insulate and save young berries. On the worst night, the 12th, the temperature dropped to 18 degrees not long after sundown and stayed there all night. Kline spent the night stumbling through the frozen plants going from sprinkler head to sprinkler head with a hammer, knocking the ice off the frozen heads to keep them working.

"I about killed myself with that ice on that old rye grass. You couldn't walk out there. You was fallin' and crawlin' more than you was walkin'. A little old sprig of rye grass like that" (Kline holds up his pointer finger) "had that much ice built up on it" (Kline holds his other hand six inches above the finger). "You can imagine fallin' on that thing and it stabbin' you in the ribs and the butt. I bet you I fell a dozen times.

"That's about the most miserable thing I've went through. I've went through some tough things, but I think that took the cake. Dark, you'd fall, couldn't get up, roll around on that ice and try to get a foot or hand hold on something. Ice sticking all over my face. My pants, when I got home, I got Garrett to help pull 'em off. They was froze solid from my knees down. There was ice froze all over my face, my hands. You wouldn't believe how I looked. I was pitiful."

The strawberry plants survived, and the first berries should be ready for picking next week.

Larry Moore suffered a stroke, underwent an operation, and spent a couple of weeks in the hospital. He's back home and recovering.

Kline has decided not to grow cotton this year after the crop he sold in March went for the low price of 62 cents a pound. The second-hand picker is parked behind one of the out-buildings on the farm, and Kline isn't looking for a newer one.

The farm's new venture is an ice cream parlor. Kline began work on it in March and thinks it will bring more customers to his retail stand. Several other growers in the state have added ice cream parlors lately, and Kline wants to give it a try.

He will be getting a high-quality ice cream from a company in Mooresville, North Carolina. "The man who owns the company came down and talked with me. He said that Kemp (McLeod) does fairly good with his."

Cindy and Vicky Brown will have to run it until the first of June before they can get some help from high-schoolers.

"Of course, by that time, I'll probably weigh 250 pounds if I get into that butter pecan ice cream," Kline says with a laugh.

The retail store has had a general makeover to make way for the ice cream, and the changes are startling. Kline and Chad have cleared out many of the old produce displays. The walls have been painted, and a new floor of black and white tiles has been laid. Vickie has been busy framing photographs and copies of old peach labels for display on the walls. Half a dozen tables and matching chairs await the customers. Kline plans to open next week.

There will be no more peaches at Sunny Slope Farms. Under the newspaper headline, "Peachy deal from Sunny Slope," Caggiano family members announced they will develop Sunny Slope Hills Golf and Country Club on the northwest corner of their land. It will have an 18-hole

Ice Cream Parlor. June, 1998.

Survey Stake. Sunny Slope Field. Battleground Road. July, 1998.

championship golf course and 350 upscale homes. They plan to auction off 600 additional acres in lots ranging from one to 15 acres. The land that fronts the interstate will be converted to an industrial park.

"I never imagined 10 years ago that we would be going out of the peach business," one of the Caggiano daughters was quoted as saying. "It's nice to see something like this happen to Cherokee County, and it's nice for us to be a part of it."

The Caggianos won't run their packing house this year, and Kline has agreed to pack their last crop.

Kline has ordered some equipment to put universal bar-code stickers on each of his packed peaches. The equipment will cost about $25,000, but Kline doesn't have much choice. "Just about every buyer has told us they won't buy any fruit without it."

Chad Cash is getting married, and the outdoor ceremony is scheduled for May. "I already told her what she was getting into, about those days when she won't hardly see me until one or two o'clock in the morning," Chad says.

When asked what he likes best about farming, Kline's reply is direct and sincere: "Gettin' outside and watching things grow. You know, all the hoopla and everything you have to go through, sometimes it's exciting, sometimes it's dull. It's always a challenge. Bottom line, the reason I stay here and farm is just to put a seed in the ground and see what you can make it produce. That's the bottom line, just watching things grow, to be close to nature."

The Cash Family. July, 1998.
Vickie, Garrett, Kline, Chad, and Cindy.

AUTHOR'S NOTE

I came late to the peach fields of Spartanburg County. My wife and I, along with a brand new son, first came to Spartanburg in 1976 to teach school. Ed Hall, a friend and colleague at one of the schools where I taught, was supervisor of the state agricultural inspection service for Spartanburg. Knowing my need for summer employment, Ed kindly invited me to join the service, and I worked at several packing houses during the peach season during the next few years.

Despite a freeze-out in 1980, those years that I inspected were busy ones for the industry. In my first season, the local office employed more than 20 inspectors, almost all teachers, coaches, or school administrators. Dozens of packing houses paid their "nickel a box" to the agriculture department for the "No. 1 Extra, USDA Inspected" stamp on the box. Most buyers and brokers required the inspections for the scores of truckloads of peaches that left Upstate packing houses daily for markets all over the East Coast, the Midwest, and Canada.

For the most part, I enjoyed those summers. The peach business was novel to me and interesting.

I met many fine people. Of all the people that I met and worked with, I grew to respect the Cash family as much as I did anyone. The family members were dedicated to what they were doing. The Cashes worked hard to pack the best peaches that they could. They rejoiced in the 14-hour July days of a successful harvest. Even when they were tired or frustrated (common events for a farmer), they treated one and all with courtesy, respect, and good humor.

I have dim memories of Woodrow Cash, mostly in poor health in those days, occasionally coming to the packing house. He sometimes would rest in the packing house in an old, caned, ladder-back chair and visit and watch the work of his children. They all were grown and raising their own families.

I stopped inspecting in the mid-eighties and became busy with other pursuits, but I still periodically stopped by Cash Farms to buy fruit. As I became more involved with photography, I often visited and took photographs.

By October 1995, when I first sat down with Kline Cash to discuss the possibility of a photo-documentation of Cash Farms, a lot of changes had taken place. Woodrow had died in 1983. Despite their best efforts, the Cash children could not make the farm pay enough to support their three families, and Barry and Gwen had left to begin other careers. Land had been sold to satisfy creditors.

With the support of a grant from the Arts Partnership of Greater Spartanburg, I began taking photographs in the winter of 1995-96. The farm had enjoyed three consecutive fairly good years, and we all hoped for another one. I envisioned that the project would record a kind of march through the seasons and culminate in the celebration of a successful harvest in 1996.

It wasn't to be. After a March freeze killed the peach crop, I continued to photograph the farm and record its efforts to survive in the face of the failure of its major crop.

As I spent more time at the farm, I became increasingly interested in recording the stories and the history. I soon found that the small notebooks I used for captions, addresses, and technical information were inadequate. I began carrying a tape recorder, making transcripts, and keeping a journal. I gradually expanded the project beyond Cash Farms and began learning more about the history of the peach industry in the Piedmont and the state.

With the support of a second grant from the Arts Partnership, I completed the documentation of the farm in July 1997. "A Year in the Life of an Upstate Peach Farm," an exhibit of many of the photographs contained in this book, debuted at the Spartanburg County Art Museum in late summer of that year.

   Vickie Cash once said that she didn't think her family "was especially interesting." I think Vickie is just plain wrong about that, and I hope some portion of what I came to admire about the Cashes is conveyed in this work. I am especially grateful to Kline for allowing me to become a semi-fixture around the farm and his family for the past two years. There were times when my presence must have been intrusive and some of my questions a chore, but each family member and employee on the farm welcomed me. Thank you, Kline, Vickie, Chad, Cindy, Garrett, and other members of the family: Gwen Cash Gray and Barry Cash, Marie Cash Belue, J.D. and Dianne Young, and "Aunt Vada" Cash Sellars. I also thank Mr. and Mrs. Jamous Cash for helping me learn more about the "Jefferson Davis" branch of the family.

   I appreciate the cooperation of the employees of Cash Farms who, with work to do, put up with me, answered all my questions, allowed me to photograph them, and never—not once—ran me over with a tractor. Thank you Vicky Brown, Walt Posey, Dick Carson, Larry Moore, and all the members of the "crew", including Lee Frazier, Roy Hambrick, Danny McCaskill, Gene McClendon, Robert Williams, Donna Moore, Willie Mae Dawkins, and Joe Paul Baldwin.

   There were many other people who generously shared their experiences with me while I was completing the photo-documentation and the research that became this book. That I was able to retell just some of their stories on these pages does not diminish the value of their contributions nor my appreciation for their patience and consideration. My heartfelt thanks to the following people and organizations: Bob Evans, Mike Mastropietro, and Paul Eaton, all of Keystone Fruit Marketing Inc., for taking the time to answer my questions about the brokering side of the business. Benji Richter of Richter and Company in Charlotte did the same and more, graciously sharing his family's history in the business.

   I am grateful to many farmers, active and retired, for sharing some part of their families' lives in the peach business. In the Piedmont: James Cooley and Cooley Farms, home of "Strawberry Hill, USA;" Bruce Johnson of Johnson Farms and BBB Packing near Inman; Henry Gramling II of Gramling Brothers; Howard and Sara Painter; Toy and Wayne Hyder of Campobello; and Ruth Hatchette

McBrayer. Also, Buck and Cozette Price of Gaffney; W. J. Sprinkles Jr.; Louis V. Caggiano and Louis Caggiano Jr. of Sunny Slope Farms; State Senator J. C. Verne Smith of Greer; and Ben and Merwyn Smith of "The Peach Tree" in York County. Bruce Woodfin of Gramling shared the written history of his family's participation in the first years of the commercial peach-growing industry in Spartanburg. Marianna Habisreutinger of the Black family of Spartanburg shared her memories of her father's farm as well as the family's "shopping bag" archives of National Peach Council annuals.

Jerry Watson of Watsonia Farms in Moneta not only showed me his family's farm but introduced me to the "Ridge" peach-growing section of South Carolina. Tracy Childers and his two sons, David and Todd, of Moneta Packing patiently answered my questions. My visit with Tom and Ann Carson Holstein at their farm near Moneta was a pleasure and an education, as was my visit with the McLeods at their farm in Chesterfield County in the Sand Hills.

Jack Brannon of Cherokee Springs eloquently shared his life-long involvement in peach farming. Arthur Johnson of Booneville, Kentucky, provided information about his retailing operation in Kentucky and Indiana.

The role of Clemson University in the growth of the peach industry in South Carolina is another story left largely untold in this book. I am deeply indebted to Greg Reighard of Clemson, who introduced me to the school's experimental fruit farm, Musser Farm. Michael Watkins of the South Carolina Seed Foundation and Edmund Taylor, a Clemson extension agent specializing in horticulture, both found time to help me.

Charles Banks and Rebecca Causey of the USDA provided valuable insights into land and farm management. Emory Price of the Spartanburg County Planning Commission generously shared his resources and experience in providing a clear understanding of past, present, and predicted development in Spartanburg. Weather data, crop statistics, and road information were provided in timely fashion by representatives of the South Carolina Department of Natural Resources, Agricultural Statistics Service, and the Department of Transportation.

Bob McCurry of the state Department of Agriculture made me feel welcome at the peach growers' 1997 convention in Augusta. Bob Ray of Robert Ray Farms in Fort Valley, Georgia, and the Georgia Peach Council helped explain the federal crop-loss insurance program. Gene Klimstra of Hendersonville, North Carolina, shared his expertise in apple farming and marketing. Phillip Pelham and Nancy Ray of Cumberland Valley Nurseries provided an understanding of the workings of their commercial tree operation in Tennessee.

Charlotte Huskey and Carolyn Creal of the Spartanburg County Historical Association generously loaned their resources. My thanks to Everett Powers, George Loudon, and the board of directors of the Arts Partnership of Greater Spartanburg for their interest, support, and understanding.

My "day job" is a demanding one—teaching art and photography at Carver Junior High School in Spartanburg. I am fortunate to work with a principal who is as understanding and supportive as Al Jeter has been these past two years.

This project would not have been possible without the constant help and patience of my family, especially that of my wife, Nancy Linn Corbin. Thank you Cai, Nate, Max, and Nancy.

Betsy Teter and Mark Olencki of the Hub City Writers Project are greatly responsible for the shape and content of this book. With patience and humor, Betsy showed a very raw author a way through hundreds of pages of notes, transcripts, and research. And as a long-time friend and admirer of Mark's work, I feel doubly honored that he agreed to design this book.

The factories and businesses, houses and golf courses, pasture and timber that now stand where peach trees once covered the rolling hillsides of the South Carolina Piedmont are not bad things. Today, more people are enjoying more opportunities and higher standards of living as a result, and more people are living longer and healthier lives.

As Kline Cash and any farmer will tell you, there is precious little that is romantic about farming. It is a hard business filled with uncertainty. Yet there is a feeling shared by many that farming is closely tied to "coming home" and of connecting with the past.

I am not a farmer, but I have many ancestors who were. All of my grandparents were raised on small farms in southern Indiana, and all left the farm as they entered adulthood in the years before World War I. There were few—if any—prosperous years on the farm, either for the Corbins or my mother's family, the Stevensons.

My grandfather, Mordecai "M. C." Corbin, attended school through the third grade, then began working full-time on the farm. The farm was so poor, he, like all of his brothers, was "farmed out" at age 12 to live at one of the bigger, more prosperous farms in the area. (The family "broke his plate," it was commonly said.) There he worked dawn to dusk for room and board and token wages until leaving farming for good at age 16.

For the many people who live in the Piedmont who were not among the thousands who worked in the peach orchards or packing houses over the years, I hope that this account of one family's peach farm will provide a small window of appreciation of those who did and for those, like the Cash family, who continue to tend the orchards.

—M.S.C.
June, 1998

ABOUT THE AUTHOR

Three generations removed from the farm, Mike Corbin grew up in Ohio and saw his first peach fields shortly after coming to Spartanburg County to teach school in 1976. He first met the Cash family when he began working as a peach inspector for the U. S. Department of Agriculture during the summers in the late seventies.

He and his wife, Nancy, have taught art for the last 20 years and have mutually enjoyed, for the most part, the on-going adventure of raising their three sons, Cai, Nathan, and Max.

Mike's day job is teaching art and photography at Carver Junior High School in Spartanburg. He also has taught photography to plenty of other students, from fifth graders in introductory workshops to adults in graduate-level college and continuing education courses.

He has had his photographs published recently in two other books about Spartanburg: *Hub City Anthology* and *Spartanburg: A Portrait of the Good Life*. *Family Trees* is his first book. It is an experience that has given him a renewed respect and admiration for the art of writing.

Nate Corbin

PHOTOGRAPHY NOTES

All photographs were taken at Cash Farms unless otherwise noted.

CHAPTER ONE

*pg*12 • **Kline Cash. March, 1997.**
    Kline inspects a peach bud one morning after the temperatures dropped below 20 degrees.

*pg*20 • **Spraying the Encores. March, 1997.**
    This block of Encore trees is planted in a "high density" pattern, with six-foot spacings between trees. As many as 400 trees can be planted this way. The traditional checkerboard planting of the open-center tree limits the number of trees to 100 to 140 per acre.

*pg*38 • **Gene McClendon. July, 1996.**
    The day after an evening rain, Gene reaches deep into a tree to pick one of the few peaches of

the season.

*pg*41 • **Kline Cash. June, 1997.**
Kline inspects the trees in the Harvester block on the first day of picking.

*pg*45 • **ORD Tractor. July, 1997.**
Donna and Sonny help fill the field bins.

*pg*46 • **Camp Wash. February, 1997.**
Harvester trees are in the background.

*pg*47 • **Day Done. July, 1996.**
Some of Larry's crew–Jesse, Greg, Sonny, and Gary–relax after a hot day's work in the field.

CHAPTER TWO

*pg*48 • **Irrigated Orchard. July, 1993.**
An overhead sprayer fed by water from a pond irrigates one of the orchards at Cash Farms.

*pg*50• **John and Alice Cash surrounded by their children. Undated.**
(Photo courtesy of the Cash family)

*pg*51 • **Kline Cash on Mule. Late 1940s.**
(Photo courtesy of the Cash family)

*pg*52 • **Alice and Chad Cash. 1973.**
Alice Cash was over 90 years old and her great-grandson, Chad, was not yet two when this photo was taken at the farm's old packing house.
(Photo courtesy of the Cash family)

*pg*54 • **Woodrow Cash. 1971.**

Woodrow Cash, right, is shown here with the old packing house in the background (the other figure is unidentified). The packing house was built where his sister, Vada, and her husband, Paul, once had their mattress factory, and it stood until 1976 when it was torn down to make way for the modern structure housing the farm's packing house, offices, and store.

(Photo courtesy of the Cash family)

*pg*55 • **Woodrow, Barry, Gwen, and Kline. Undated.**

This photo was probably taken in the 1970s at the old packing house when Woodrow and his children were still working the farm together.

(Photo courtesy of the Cash family)

*pg*57 • **Mt. Vernon Farm Packing House. Greer, S.C. 1914.**

J. Verne Smith, the "pioneer peach grower of the Piedmont," is on the far left.

(Photo courtesy of the Smith family)

*pg*59 • **The Taylor Brothers in Mt. Vernon Orchard. Greer, S.C. 1930s.**

The Taylor brothers–Earl, Beco, Spartan, and Albert–are pictured in a break from "shaking for curculios." They would spread a sheet under each tree and shake the tree until the small, plum curculio beetles would fall on the sheet and be exterminated.

(Photo courtesy of the Smith family)

*pg*61 • **Early Commercial Orchard. Spartanburg County. 1925.**

Many of the men involved in the county's young industry were attending a pruning demonstration when this photograph was taken: A.E. Schilletter, Judge Gentry, Count Culbreth, George Settle, Claude Bishop, Bill Tinsley, Landon Edgar Reeder, Ernest Carnes, B. M. Gramling, P. J. Woodfin, M. F. Johnson, John Turpin, and John Tinsley.

(Photo courtesy of Henry Gramling II and Bruce Woodfin)

*pg*62 • **Toy Hyder. Campobello, S.C. January, 1997.**

During Toy Hyder's boyhood in the 1920s, cotton wagons pulled by mules filled the yard and his family's gin yard. They stretched out of sight down the road. The original cotton scales are still in Toy's office and can be seen in the background in this photo.

Toy's father planted his first peach trees in the thirties and the farm gradually made the transition from cotton to peaches over the next couple of decades. The last bale of cotton ginned on the place was in 1960.

After returning from World War II, Toy helped run the South Carolina Peach Growers Association for many years and marketed the co-op's "Palmetto Queen" brand of peaches.

Toy and his son, Wayne, still have about 175 acres of peaches, and in 1998, Wayne opened a new retail stand on Highway 11 near Gowensville.

Once, upon hearing that a 90-year-old man in the community was putting out new peach trees, Toy announced, "Now *that* is a definition of an optimist."

*pg*63 • **Hyder Packing House. Campobello, S.C. April, 1997.**

The Hyders closed down this packing house after the 1993 season and had neighboring farmers pack the fruit. Originally built in 1898 for cotton seed storage, the building was converted to pack peaches in the 1930s.

*pg*64 • **Brannon and Brannon Packing House. Highway 9, Spartanburg County. March, 1997.**

This is one of the many closed or converted packing houses in the Piedmont. It was closed in the 1960s.

*pg*66 • **Spartanburg Peach Monument. June, 1997.**

This monument was erected in the city of Spartanburg in 1947 across from Cleveland Park on what is now called Berry Field.

*pg*67 • **1953 National Peach Council Annual.**

The cover of the annual showed her "Majesty The Queen of Fruits" enthroned at the head ban-

quet table at the Spartanburg Memorial Auditorium.
(Annual courtesy of Marianna Habisreutinger)

*pg*68-69 • **Field Crews. Spartanburg County. 1930s.**
The early peach industry was a labor-intensive and segregated enterprise. These two crews worked trees owned by the Woodfin family near Gramling.
(Photos courtesy of Bruce Woodfin)

*pg*70 • **Scene from outside Woodfin Shed. Spartanburg County. 1930s.**
(Photo courtesy of Bruce Woodfin)

*pg*71 • **Time Sheet. 1935.**
This page from the Woodfin Farm weekly time book recorded an hourly wage of 15 cents per hour.

*pg*72 • **"I am a tree!" Kline Cash at Watsonia Farms. Moneta, S.C. January, 1997.**
After attending the Peach Growers Convention in Augusta, Georgia, Chad and Kline stopped off at the Watson family farm in the "Ridge" section of the state to demonstrate their pruning methods for high-density pattern orchards. Here is Kline's best impersonation of a correct-growth axis for each of the tree's opposing limbs.

*pg*76 • **Jerry Gaines. Inman, S.C. July, 1998.**
The Gaines family first operated this packing house in 1954. Jerry reports that his busiest year was 1995 when the farm shipped 100,000 boxes of peaches. Although the shed was closed in 1996 and 1997, it reopened in 1998 and was one of only four operating in the South Carolina Piedmont.

*pg*77 • **Ned and Woodrow Potter. Potter Store. Cowpens, S.C. May, 1997.**
The Potter family has known and done business with several generations of the Cash family from this general store in Cowpens. Woodrow, now 87 years old, first worked in the store in 1927. In turn, his son, Ned, joined him and has worked his entire adult life there.

Shortly after this photo was taken, the Potters sold the store. The new owner plans to restore it and apply to have the building placed on the National Register of Historic Places.

CHAPTER THREE

*pg*78 • **Chad Cash. January, 1997.**

*pg*83 • **Ladders. Sunny Slope Farms. April, 1997.**
When Kline Cash saw this picture, he said, "There's only one place this could be. It has to be Sunny Slope. They're the only ones that have that many ladders."

*pg*85 • **Louis V. Caggiano, Sr. Sunny Slope Farms. June, 1997.**
"My dad first brought me down here in 1936 and that's how I got involved in it. I was only 16 years old. We started with 80 acres in 1943. We grew to about 2,000 acres. We've loved it."

*pg*88 • **Yeah, Baby! Chad Cash. June, 1997.**
The night before the packing house opened for the season, Chad had a friend give him a new haircut. His mother, Vickie, who normally cuts the hair of the men in her family wasn't pleased to see what her eldest son had done to his head.

*pg*91 • **Sampling. July, 1997.**
Mike Mastropietro samples a box of peaches in Cash Farms' smaller cooler.

*pg*96 • **Hatchette's Peach Shed. Highway 11 and Dillon Street. December, 1996.**
The last year of operation for this packing house was 1984. Built in 1945, it was the last packing house in Upstate South Carolina to still use ice for the hydro-cooler.

*pg*98 • **Packing. June, 1996.**
The peaches come out of the water bath after being dumped from a field bin and are moved by

rollers to the grading station inside the packing house.

CHAPTER FOUR

*pg*110 • **December Cotton. McBrayer Field. Highway 11 & Battleground Road. December, 1996.**

*pg*114 • **Irrigation Pipes. July, 1996.**
In the midst of a three-week drought, Brent and Chad lay out sections of pipe to irrigate a cornfield.

*pg*115 • **Cornfield, Irrigation. July, 1996.**
This field has since been planted in "Big Red" peach trees. Cash Farms did not plant any corn in 1997.

*pg*116 • **Dick Carson. October, 1996.**
Dick had badly scratched his right eye on a tree branch. It had almost completely healed at this time.

*pg*122 • **Chad Cash. November, 1996.**
Chad is in the farm's garage, grinding down a small part, a "key lock" for the cotton picker. Chad became the designated cotton picker mechanic and, by necessity, would learn a lot more than he really cared to know about the workings of the old machine during the next two years.

*pg*123 • **Spindles, Cotton Picker. November, 1996.**
The basic component of the cotton picker is the spindle. Each about the size of a little finger, the stainless steel spindles are studded with dozens of small, slightly raised teeth or barbs, all biased at an angle to the spindle's axis. Run your fingers over the barbs in one direction, and they feel slightly bumpy. Try to run your fingers the other way, and the teeth will grab and tear the skin.
When the picker is operating, hundreds of these spindles spin around the drums at 900 RPMs

inside the mouth of the picker, stripping the cotton bolls and seed from the rows of plants in the field.

EPILOGUE

*pg*126 • **The Hands of Aunt Vada. Battleground Road. October, 1996.**
    Vada was at her kitchen table by a window overlooking Battleground Road and the Cash Farms strawberry patch.

*pg*131 • **Survey Stake. Sunny Slope Field. Battleground Road. July, 1998.**
    The land is being prepared for a golf course and upscale residential development.

Publication of *Family Trees* has been made possible by generous contributions from

Susu and George Dean Johnson

In honor of

Lois Dean Gilmartin, Mary Burgin Presnell Montgomery, and Sara Carson Phifer

Three Spartanburg women who left no heirs but great legacies

and:

The Arts Partnership of Greater Spartanburg

Mr. and Mrs. Robert Allen
Mr. and Mrs. Stan Baker
Dianne and Jim Bagnal
Mr. and Mrs. John Bancer
Thomas Barnes and Ekky Foss
Mr. and Mrs. William Barnet
Mr. and Mrs. Joe Betras
Linda and Victor Bilanchone
Mr. and Mrs. Glen B. Boggs II
Beatrice and Dennis Bruce
Mellnee G. Buchheit
Carolina Southern Foundation
Mr. and Mrs. Arthur Cleveland
Barbara and John Cobb
Barbara Stevenson Corbin
Suellen Dean
John Carl Dennis
Mr. and Mrs. Frederick B. Dent. Jr.
Ann and Michael Eickman
The Rev. Beth Ely
Mr. and Mrs. Michael D. Franke

Mr. and Mrs. Charles H. Gray Jr.
Hanh-Trang and Gerald Ginocchio
Mr. and Mrs. Roger Habisreutinger
T. Winston Hardegree
Curtis Harley
Agnes Harris
Daniel J. and Jami A. Harrison
Toy and Wayne Hyder
Lisa Isenhower
Albert Jeter
Dorothy and Julian Josey
Johnson Farms Inc.
Jay Kaplan
Lavon Kelley
Barbara Latham
Dennis and Linda Linn
George Loudon
Dr and Mrs. Nathanial F. Magruder
Carlabeth Mathias
Jane B. May
Thomas and Susan McDaniel
Dr. Dean McKinney

McLeod Farms Inc.
Mr. and Mrs. E. Lewis Miller
Suzanne and Dennis Mitchell
Dr. and Mrs. Kirk Neely
Olencki Graphics Inc.
Dr. and Mrs. Neil Parnes
Mr. and Mrs. Dwight Patterson
Mr. and Mrs. John Poole
Everett Powers
The Refshauge Family
Barbara K. Rumple &
Rainbow Circle Farm
Beth Sabin
The Jon Emmett and Virginia H.
Shuler Fund
Mr. and Mrs. J. Verne Smith
Stephen Stinson
Dudley and Vicky Strange
Wallace and Jan Taylor
Cynthia and Colin Urquhart
Michael and Susan Vank

Publication of this book is funded in part by the Arts Partnership of Greater Spartanburg and its donors, the County and City of Spartanburg, and the South Carolina Arts Commission which receives support from the National Endowment for the Arts. All proceeds from the sale of this book go to the Hub City Writers Project.

The Hub City Writers Project is a non-profit organization whose mission is to foster a sense of community through the literary arts. We do this by publishing books from and about our community; encouraging, mentoring, and advancing the careers of local writers; and seeking to make Spartanburg a center for the literary arts.

Our metaphor of organization purposely looks backward to the nineteenth century when Spartanburg was known as the "hub city," a place where railroads converged and departed.

As we approach the twenty-first century, Spartanburg is fast becoming a literary hub of South Carolina with an active and nationally celebrated core group of poets, fiction writers, and essayists. We celebrate these writers—and the ones yet born—as one of our community's greatest assets. William R. Ferris, former director of the Center for the Study of Southern Cultures, says of the emerging South, "Our culture is our greatest resource. We can shape an economic base . . . And it won't be an investment that will disappear."

Hub City Anthology • John Lane & Betsy Teter, editors
Hub City Music Makers • Peter Cooper
Hub City Christmas • John Lane & Betsy Teter, editors
New Southern Harmonies • Rosa Shand, Scott Gould, Deno Trakas, George Singleton
The Best of Radio Free Bubba • Meg Barnhouse, Pat Jobe, Kim Taylor, Gary Phillips

COLOPHON

Family Trees was grown, pruned, and packaged with a new look for 1998. The 10" x 8" format was nurtured on our "tried and true" and now fully-operational Power Macintosh® 7100/80, with all 4.3 gigs of storage, 132 megs of RAM, a Polaroid SprintScan 35 Plus®, ZIP® and JAZ® drives, Adobe® PageMaker® 6.5 and PhotoShop® 4.0, and the soon-to-be upgraded MacOS 7.5. An almost identical CPU was added to this torpid but trustworthy system. It was used as a scan-only workstation to speed up the book's production. This second PowerPC® has somewhat less storage (1.5 gigs), another ZIP® drive for the "sneaker-network," the almost extinct but highly prized HP ScanJet IIcx®, and the much-needed Norton AntiVirus® 5.0 for those pesky "autostart worms." A first edition and printing of 2000 soft-bound and a limited edition of 150 case-bound copies exist to date. The Garamond family from ITC was used as the text typefaces; GrecoDeco Solid was the display face with help from its kin GrecoDeco Inline as the dropcaps and chapter numerals. GrailLight appears as the diary dates. Murray McDavid®, a 1987 Laphroaig® production, was hand- delivered to this country from Scotland by the editors to assist the designer in the wee hours of the production mornings. Alas, several good thoughts and PageMaker® files fell victim to "this heavy, pungent whisky that takes no prisoners." However, unlike one of the founders "whom came to grief at the bottom of a fermenting vat," this designer has learned valuable life-lessons at a much lower price.